RETHINKING ANARCHY
direct action, autonomy, self-management

carlos taibo

translated by the autonomies collective

Rethinking Anarchy: Direct Action, Autonomy, Self-Management

© 2019 Carlos Taibo

Translation © 2019 The Autonomies | autonomies.org

This edition © 2019 AK Press (Chico, Edinburgh)
ISBN: 978-1-84935-332-8
E-ISBN: 978-1-84935-333-5
Library of Congress Control Number: 2018932265

AK Press   AK Press
370 Ryan Ave. #100   33 Tower St.
Chico, CA 95973   Edinburgh EH6 7BN
USA   Scotland
www.akpress.org   www.akuk.com
akpress@akpress.org   ak@akedin.demon.co.uk

The above addresses would be delighted to provide you with the latest AK
Press distribution catalog, which features books, pamphlets, zines, and
stylish apparel published and/or distributed by AK Press. Alternatively,
visit our websites for the complete catalog, latest news, and secure
ordering.

Cover and interior design by Margaret Killjoy | birdsbeforethestorm.net

Printed in the USA

CONTENTS

PROLOGUE

It is strikingly evident that we are witnessing a remarkable renewal of libertarian ideas and practices. The corresponding movements, which have often been taken for dead, demonstrate a surprising capacity for survival that is ultimately sustained by an undeniable fact: we stand before a current of thought and action whose constant presence can be verified since time immemorial. The interest in anarchism is growing at a moment when the word *crisis* resounds everywhere, along with a growing awareness of the terminal corrosion of capitalism and the general collapse that may accompany it. And it is becoming increasingly obvious that the discourse of capital—there is no alternative other than our own, they tell us—is crumbling. There are ever more people who take notice of this and ask in vain for some explanation about the presumed suitability of that which, given the evidence, no longer has any.

The perception of what constitutes anarchism's virtues and flaws has changed continuously, often notably, over the course of time—in particular over the last quarter-century with the collapse of social democracy and Leninism. Many appear to have been mistaken, especially those who saw in anarchism a project completely incapable of addressing the problems of complex societies. The arguments today appear farcical; arguments that continue to be repeated, which suggest that anarchism is a worldview of the past, only imaginable—whatever these terms may mean—in the minds of simple people who inhabit backward countries. And it is surprising that there are people who fail to appreciate greater problems with growth, industrialization, centralization, mass consumption, competition, and military discipline. Anarchism does indeed imply restoring many of the characteristic elements of particular communities of the past, but it also involves an effort at a complex understanding of the miseries of the present, venturing in favor of self-management, decommodification, and an awareness of limits.

None of the above should be taken to mean that libertarian thought offers answers to all our concerns, much less that an *aggiornamento* is unnecessary—something that at times seems to be indispensable. We are obliged to rethink, or to qualify, many of the concepts that we have inherited from the nineteenth-century *classics*. We urgently need to adapt anarchist thought to new realities, even more so when the problems it identified a century or a century and a half ago—authoritarianism, oppression, exploitation—have in no way abated. In some sense, we find ourselves before two interrelated paradoxes. The first one reminds us that, while anarchism encounters unquestionably serious difficulties in positioning itself within the societies in which unfortunately it has been our lot to live, there seems to be a growing necessity to confront the calamities of these very societies. The second one underscores the evident weakness of those organizations that claim an *anarchist* identity, in contrast to a remarkable and more general influence of the *libertarian* project.

Therefore it appears ever more pressing to break with the isolation inherent in many identitarian forms of anarchism and to consequently do so from the nondogmatic perspective of those who are necessarily doubtful and who know that they do not hold—and I will say this again—the answers to everything. We must face the tension between the inescapable radicalness of the ideas we advocate and the knowledge that these ideas ought to reach out to many human beings and have practical consequences. Unsatisfied with what we are, convinced of our necessity, and conscious of the glories and the miseries of the past, it often becomes clear that we talk a lot, but we do not act in a desirable manner.

What I refer to above is the mental scenario wherein this book unfolds, which incidentally is a breviary due to its being a compendium of reduced dimensions and not through an imagined pretense that includes some sort of liturgical wisdom. Several years ago, I submitted to print an anthology of libertarian thought that aimed mainly at rescuing texts by the *classics*, who as far as I'm concerned, shed light on many of the challenges we must now face.[1] That is certainly not the aim of this modest volume the reader has in her hands. In no way do I pretend to address in these pages the various debates surrounding such pluralist and complex thought as the anarchist idea. I am content to offer some material open to discussion—never a hermetic and unquestionable text—directed first and foremost to those individuals who possess some kind of militant experience, or a knowledge of it, within social movements or unions, material whose objective is essentially to reflect on what we have done so far, the stigmas we have been cursed with—individualists, hostile to all sort of organization, chiliastics, infantile prepoliticals, et cetera—and

---

1 *Libertari@s. Antología de anarquistas y afines para uso de las generaciones jóvenes* (Barcelona: Del Lince, 2010).

what we are supposed to do. So, in case it is not sufficiently evident to the reader, I would like to clarify that this book is in no way an introduction to anarchism that may assess, for instance, the differences between mutualists, collectivists, and communists. It is neither a post-anarchist nor a post-structuralist text, much less a postmodern one, however much it feigns perspectives influenced by a weary zeal upon certainties and established truths as well as an express design to consider at all times the multiple forms of exploitation and alignment that torment us.

This may be the appropriate moment, then, to warn about a terminological choice that permeates most of this work. Although the adjectives *anarchist* and *libertarian* will be taken as synonyms throughout and in such a way that they may be employed without any distinction whatsoever, more often than not—as I will explain later on—I will reserve the latter to portray positions and movements that are not necessarily anarchist but that nonetheless agree with basic tenets, like those linked to direct democracy, assemblies, or self-management. When I make use of such meaning, the usage of the adjective *anarchist* will remain circumscribed to the description of positions and movements that assume a clear doctrinal identification with anarchism, understood in its most restricted sense.

During the task of writing of this work, I have consulted some of the material I have been publishing over the last few years, which has been heavily edited for the current volume; namely, the chapter "A vueltas con el Estado del bienestar: espacios de autonomía y desmercantilización," from the collective effort *¡Espabilemos! Argumentos desde el 15-M* (Madrid: Los Libros de la Catarata, 2012); the epigraph "Un capitalismo en corrosión terminal," from my book *España, un gran país: Transición, milagro y quiebra* (Madrid: Los Libros de la Catarata, 2012); the text "Ciudadanismo y movimientos sociales," which appeared in the May 2013 bulletin of the Fundación Anselmo Lorenzo; and the articles "La CNT cumple cien años," "Los modelos latinoamericanos: una re-flexión libertaria," and "Por qué hay que construir espacios autónomos," which I have published on my website, www.carlostaibo.com, in October 2010 and in April and May 2013, respectively.

—Carlos Taibo

I.

ABOUT ANARCHISM

What Anarchism Is

GIVEN THAT ANARCHISM has a manifestly antidogmatic outlook, it is hardly surprising that determining what anarchism
proper is ends up being a singularly complex task. There exist
two distinct perceptions relative to it, if you will. The first
asserts that anarchism refers to a state of mind that, sustained
by a way of seeing the world, manifests itself through behav-
ior that sinks its roots into time immemorial, whereas the second relates to a specific doctrine with clearly defined outlines
that saw the light of day at the end of the eighteenth and the
beginning of the nineteenth centuries.

In regard to the first of these perceptions, we should not
forget that by the end of the eighteenth century the adjective
anarchist had been commonly employed to describe earlier

peoples and initiatives. This usage of the term been evident in references to Chinese peasants, members of religious movements in Medieval Europe, or specific forms of piracy, to name a few among many examples.[1] The label has also framed accounts of the condition of *primitive societies*, such as the Nuer peoples studied by Evans-Pritchard, the Piaroa considered by Overing, or the many peoples invoked in the writings of Sahlins and Clastres. Acknowledging this condition seems to have an important consequence in regard to determining what should be of interest to an eventual history of anarchism. The latter should not only address the relatively recent evolution of certain ideas but should also approach the condition and the deployment of many human initiatives recorded in the distant past, for—according to this perspective—in the general body of anarchism, practices hold greater relevance than theoretical reflections.

It is also true that there exist important links between the two perceptions of anarchism that I have so poorly glossed. For instance, in the eyes of some historians, anarchism was little more than a passing and extemporaneous manifestation of so-called primitive rebels. From this perspective, the past invoked by the first of our perceptions would then burden the content of the doctrine located at the heart of the second to such a degree that the result could be nothing more than a useless jumble. This does not seem to be the best moment to address such nonsense. I will simply argue that, seen from a distance, if the primitive rebels appear preferable to their modern inheritors, it should be emphasized that the historical practice of anarchism is open to anything and includes frequent manifestations in complex societies. I would also question the primitive condition of people who, like Noam Chomsky or Bertrand Russell, have identified themselves—with or without reason—with

---

1   For an example of the singularity of libertarian literature, see Peter Lamborn Wilson, *Pirate Utopias, Moorish Corsairs and European Renegades* (Brooklyn: Autonomedia, 2003).

anarchism, or recall that, according to my understanding, the answers offered by anarchism to many of our current problems are much more sound than those forged by its ideological competitors. Thus, despite anarchism being, indeed, a state of mind, the latter is accompanied by a body of ideas and shared experiences, though often with vague and even contradictory features. In this body of ideas and experiences we often find a lucid and reflective discourse that thereby compels us to be wary of a very common image of anarchism as an amorphous thing burdened by its emotional and irrational condition, impulsive and novelesque, romantic and prone to dejection. Yet, just as I have suggested when speaking of primitive rebels, what is wrong with emotion, especially when it is permeated by rational elements?

In the end, it would seem fitting to understand anarchism as the product of a sort of mixture of those two glossed perceptions, held together by the idea that there is ultimately a memory that conveys values and experiences in such a way that neither, despite temporal lapses and appearances, ceases to exist. The configuration of anarchism as a practice/doctrine calls on a whole tradition—one that took shape in the last two centuries around phalansteries, communes, soviets, factory councils, collectivizations, or French Mays—that, though more often than not possessing modest historical resonance, scarce concretizations, and a precarious consolidation in time, carries with it examples that shine amid a magma of misfortunes. This tradition would certainly have significance when attempting to explain certain current phenomena. It is worth bringing up in this regard a fairly widespread view that considers a movement like the fifteenth of May (15-M) as a response, among us, and in one of its forms, that is fed simultaneously from three decentralizing traditions—the local, the nationalist and the anarchist—that have deep roots in the political culture of the country where it originated.[2]

---

2   15-M is the name of a decentralized anti-austerity movement in Spain

The propensity to *live in the past*, which is not uncommon in many of the expressions of libertarian culture, may have been at the origin of the idea that anarchism itself is an ideology of the past. Therefore it is necessary to stress that the majority of anarchists do not celebrate any nostalgic attachment to the past. While, on the one hand, they simply base their assumptions on the conviction that the libertarian tradition provides extremely useful tools to think and to change what lies before us today, on the other hand, they demonstrate an awareness of an undeniable fact: if we accept the first of the perceptions under consideration here—the one that essentially sees anarchism as a type of conduct—it is inevitable to conclude that there are many and very diverse interpretations of the precise meaning of this conduct. Some of these interpretations do in fact lead to equivocations and simplifications, like those woven around individuals who are just unhappy with the existing political or economic realities in which they are obliged to live, who act under the cover of an ephemeral reaction of a merely aesthetic nature and in which immediate circumstances are overly accentuated.

The Doctrinal Body

Be that as it may, it does not seem too difficult to establish the principal elements that have molded the doctrinal body of anarchism: the rejection of all forms of authority and exploitation, (among them, those constructed around capital and the state), the defense of societies based on equality and liberty, and the consequent postulation of free association from below.

Certainly, anarchists have frequently defined themselves first on the basis of what they reject—the state, capitalism, inequality, patriarchal society, war, militarism, repression in

---

that began with protests on May 15, 2011. It is also referred to as the Indignados movement. [editor]

all its forms, authority—rather than on what they have defended as an alternative. As a result—and following an argument that merits attention—there have been some who have understood that anarchism, which has boasted a noteworthy sagacity at identifying problems and flaws, has not always been on the same hoped-for level when it has come to offering effective solutions. Even though the argument has some basis, it is worth offering a direct response: more often than not, competing worldviews cannot even assume their capacity to identify problems and flaws.

Ultimately, libertarian thinkers have often had to confront a considerable number of equivocations and misunderstandings. In fact, to take but one example, they have made a notable effort to emphasize that anarchism in no way rejects organization but rather its coercive manifestations, such as those embodied by states, armies, churches, or businesses. What this implies, at least in principle—I will admit that the case is more complicated than it might appear—is that anarchists abide by the authority of doctors, architects, or engineers.

Antidogmatic

It is important to underline that anarchism, along with its doctrinal positions, assumes—or should assume—a nondogmatic position in all areas of life. There is no principle that cannot be debated, not even its own. In this respect, it is useful to recall the words of Tomás Ibáñez: "To recognize the extreme fragility of anarchism is to perhaps demonstrate a greater anarchist sensibility than to endeavor to deny it or unwillingly admit it. It is precisely because of its *imperfection* that anarchism situates itself at the level that it pretends to occupy."[3]

---

3 Tomás Ibañez, *Actualidad del anarquismo* (La Plata/Buenos Aires: Terramar/Anarres, 2007), 93.

Anarchists have always shown a manifest concern regarding the closed programs that so please those who usually have never succeeded in realizing any program whatsoever or, what is more, have corrupted them with parties and institutions. They do not carry the burden of any pretension to construct a scientific theory, since accepting this would also imply, in one way or another, the acceptance of an authority that takes on the task of managing it. Thus, as David Graeber has suggested in many of his writings, anarchism rather represents a kind of inspirational and creative impulse that seeks to preserve—I would add—an open attitude before diversity and difference, despite knowing full well how difficult it is to impose nonimposition. In this regard, it is suspicious of any norms with universal application.[4]

The consequence of all of this has very often been an eclectic and plural thought, against the commonly homogeneous and monolithic condition of Marxist doctrine.[5] Josep Termes has in fact empashized that the Spanish libertarian movement had a multiform character, such that anarchist doctrines often functioned as a sort of background that failed to hide the primacy of working-class action led in a reasonably autonomous manner by the workers themselves.[6] Jacinto Toryho has added, "Whoever believes that what is called anarchism in Spain is a conscious anarchism, theoretically grounded in the great anarchist thinkers' doctrines, is mistaken; with very few exceptions, the great masses and the leadership possessed nothing other than a revolutionary instinct."[7] Furthermore, among Spanish libertarians, attention was accorded to both

---

4   David Graeber, *Direct Action: An Ethnography* (Oakland: AK Press, 2009), 221.

5   Josep Termes, *Història del moviment anarquista a Espanya (1870–1980)* (Barcelona: L'Avenç, 2011), 172.

6   Ibid., 20.

7   Jacinto Toryho, quoted in Termes, *Història del moviment anarquista a Espanya*, 20.

disparate and original positions: as Termes reminds us once again, the corresponding subculture found sustenance in neo-Malthusianism and birth control, sexology clinics, naturalism, nudism, vegetarianism, and Esperantism.[8]

The Learned and the Sciences

I have already noted that libertarian thought has never aspired to develop a science destined to identify, for example, an eventual and deterministic development of society. The issue, though, is not only limited to this: libertarian thought has always exhibited a notable suspicion toward the learned and intellectuals.

Bakunin, for instance, always maintained a distance from savants, intellectuals, and scientists, and in this regard, particularly contested the Comtian goal of elaborating a "scientific government" or the Marxist aim of creating a similar form of rule under "scientific socialism." (Of course, the elaboration of this last concept owes more to Engels than to Marx, who often defended a radical critique of the supposed wisdom of science.) It is true, however, that many nineteenth-century anarchists, with Proudhon heading a list that also includes Bakunin, defended the rigor of science as a counterweight to religion, even as they remained cautious about the former. Kropotkin, for his part, was always very elusive regarding the virtues attributed to science. Today it can be stated that a reasonably skeptical attitude continues to prevail in relation to the learned, the intellectuals, and the scientists in libertarian discourse, both in its doctrinal expression as well as in its concrete realizations.

To further clarify the anarchist perspective, we should recall that the collectivizations that took place during the Spanish Civil War were not planned by scientists and intellectuals, but were rather carried out by ordinary people

---

8 Termes, *Història del moviment anarquista a Espanya*, 27.

apparently deprived of knowledge. The precarious relation
between Spanish libertarians, who gave shape to a movement
with obvious popular roots, and the intellectual world is
still to be studied. However much one invokes the youthful
years of Azorín, Camba, and Maetzu or the episodic spasms
of Sender and Léon Felipe, something distanced one reality from the other. This is so much the case that only with
the passage of time did Spanish anarcho-syndicalism accept,
though with reticence, the development of labor unions created for professional intellectuals. In short, it is significant
that the majority of the *theorists* of Spanish anarchism—with
the exceptions of Tarrida del Mármol, Salvochea, Mella,
Puente, Abad de Santillán, and the members of the Urales
family—were self-taught workers.[9]

Schools and Currents

When speaking of the doctrinal body of anarchism, we must
also take into account its many schools and currents. There
are individualist anarchists, and there are those—the majority; that is, mutualists, collectivists, communists, et cetera—
who are not. There are anarchists who appeal to the people
in general, and there are those who link their demands to a
specific human group. There are anarchists who give overwhelming priority to union work, and there are those who
distrust this. There are pacifist anarchists, and there those
who are less so. There are anarchists who adhere to a flexible discursive doctrine, and also those who find vitality in
a working-class current or who collaborate with the world
of counterculture. Lastly, and appealing to a classification
that has found some echo, there are anarchists with capital
A—those who do not make up any of the aforementioned
currents—and anarchists with small *a*—those that do belong
to a given current. All of this hinders the development of a

9   Ibid., 17.

thorough criticism of anarchism, for those possibly affected may not feel concerned by it.

Nevertheless, the existence of distinct schools has seldom provoked remarkable debates. This is due to the majority of these schools lacking the same degree of confrontation that is revealed, for example, between the different currents that claim allegiance to Marx's thought, allegiances commonly portrayed by the use of one or another political leader or thinker's names. Therefore the distinction between mutualists, collectivists, and communists does not have in anarchism the same significance than the one separating Leninists, Trotskyists, and Maoists in the ideological tradition of Marxism. Neither is found in anarchism a personal icon clearly placed above others; in particular, there is no *Marx*, as there is no canonical text on the scale of *The Communist Manifesto* or *Capital*.

However much this remains the case, and even though no Bakuninists or Kropotkinists exist today, it would be absurd to deny that the individuals who give their names to such adherences continue to carry considerable weight—something perhaps inadvisable within the libertarian world and its iconoclasm. It is also seldom considered that the principal theorists of nineteenth-century anarchism were often contradictory thinkers, hostages to their times, with regard to, for instance, the issues raised by women, science, technology, or natural resources. We may perhaps be permitted to conclude that we have made some progress in this respect over the last few years, especially when it becomes evident that those considered to be the most important contemporary anarchist theorists do not possess the same aura than the great figures of the nineteenth and early twentieth centuries, such as Proudhon, Bakunin, Kropotkin, Flores Magón, Ferrer i Guàrdia, or Malatesta.

Let us agree that, as things stand, it is quite rare, in a debate between libertarians, that there is any value put on discussing whether Bakunin or Kropotkin said this or that. Given that contemporary anarchism is a complex mix of sensibilities, instead of referring to what was said by the classics, it is more common to interpret and infer what they might say today, without any major concern for fidelity. In this sense, and even if one may appreciate the rational classification of knowledge carried out by Paul Eltzbacher in his work *Anarchism* (an example among many others), the result is somewhat sterile when seen from our vantage point.[10]

Anarchists and Libertarians

In the pages above, I have indistinctly employed—and I will continue to do so in the majority of the following sections of this book—the adjectives *anarchist* and *libertarian*, albeit, as one may observe, with clear preeminence to the former. For a long time, the two adjectives have been taken as almost perfect synonyms. When one spoke of, for example, the *Catalan libertarian movement*, it was obvious that one was speaking of the *Catalan anarchist movement*. Yet I do not believe that it would be a mistake to state that these adjectives do indeed exhibit some difference. It would seem that the former, *anarchist*, carries with it a greater ideological and doctrinal weight than the latter, *libertarian*. Someone may be considered an anarchist because they have read Bakunin, Kropotkin, and Malatesta, and adhere, to some extent, to the ideas expressed by these authors. Yet the ideological and doctrinal current weakens somewhat with the adjective *libertarian*, which has a less-defined identitarian dimension and thus easily allows for a reference to people who claim to believe in direct democracy, assemblies, and self-management without being necessarily anarchist.

I would like to clarify that, although I consider reading Bakunin, Kropotkin, and Malatesta to be highly

---

10 Paul Eltzbacher, *Anarchismus* (Berlin: J. Guttentag, 1900). See also Jean Préposiet, *Histoire de l'anarchisme* (Paris: Pluriel, 2012) and George Woodcock, *Anarchism* (Harmondsworth: Penguin, 1975).

commendable, I am more interested in the nonidentitarian mental horizon that is tied to the meaning I attribute to the adjective *libertarian*—a debatable one, I must admit. In other words, I am more interested in the organizations and the people that adjust to the meaning that this adjective invokes than in the organizations and the people that meticulously adhere to the anarchist canon, underscoring my conviction that the latter more often than not dare act without any strict adherence to doctrine or identity. In line with my terminological distinction, however, I firmly believe that not all libertarians are simultaneously anarchists, but there's clearly a majority of anarchists who consequently accept the rules of the game of libertarian practice.

In early 2011, I wrote a text in which I defended the necessity of forming a libertarian and global organization that could welcome whoever declared their commitment to direct democracy, assemblies, and self-management, regardless of their *ideological* position or even lacking any such position.[11] And even though I continue to believe in the good sense of this idea, I confess that its foundations were shaken when, a few months later, the May 15 movement emerged. Above all, it was a matter of choosing between what was destined to be little more than a libertarian circle—the proposal of the article—and the prospect of preparing an organization of self-management that would break molds and boundaries. Therefore, regardless of the deficiencies of the 15-M movement, which were undoubtedly many, I stand with the libertarians and with the anarchists, who preferred to work with the movement rather than foster coteries. They preferred to work with ordinary people rather than sustain a closed and self-centered circuit. Many friends, wary of identitarian projects and the dogmas and legacies that often weigh upon them, were no doubt thankful.

---

11 "Por una organización libertaria y global," January 17, 2011, http://www.carlostaibo.com.

Yet I cannot hide the fact that these terminological options I propose carry their own problems. I will leave aside those issues stemming from the fact that it is difficult, very difficult, *to be an anarchist*. To define oneself in this way, some might think, means raising the bar too high and engaging in an exercise of inadvisable arrogance. I remember that many years ago, in 1976, on the occasion of a rally organized by the Confederación Nacional del Trabajo (CNT—National Confederation of Labor) in Manzanares, Ciudad Real, someone asked one of my fellow bus companions if he was an anarchist. Replying with a modesty not devoid of irony, he said he was "un acratilla" ("a little anarchist"). On the other hand, the not so subtle identification of *anarchy* with *disorder*, so pleasing to the makers of public opinion, fortunately does not seem to have made much progress among us.

Greater are the problems the term *libertarian* entails. The main issue is born of a well-known fact: in North American political culture, the adjective *libertarian* refers to a kind of extreme liberalism, individualistic and possessive. Although today this meaning of the term has gained some currency among us, I do not believe that, at least for the moment, it has served to fully push aside the sense of collectivity and solidarity that have always distinguished our *libertarians/anarchists*. It is worth mentioning that one of meanings of the adjective *libertarian*, very common in Latin America—associated with the actions of the *liberators* of the early nineteenth century—barely poses any problem regarding my terminological distinction.

Mutual Invigorations

The contributions of anarchists and their movements have been many and very significant. But the reverberations of their theorizations and corresponding practices spread noticeably when we include those put forth by individuals—following the terminological distinction already discussed—who get their inspiration, more generally, from the libertarian tradition.

These reverberations reveal themselves in a variety of disciplines. With no desire to present a final summary, I will refer to examples in pedagogy (Ivan Illich, Alexander S. Neill), psychiatry (David Cooper, Ronald Laing), geography (Élisée Reclus, Peter Kropotkin), anthropology (Marshall Sahlins and Pierre Clastres, referred to above), epistemology (Paul K. Feyerabend, whose work we welcomed openly four decades ago, without fully understanding its significance), and the critique of technology (Lewis Mumford, John Zerzan) or of *the other exploitations* (Cornelius Castoriadis, Michel Foucault, and, once again, Illich).

However, it is also important to refer to the mutual invigorations that libertarian thought and movements of greater or less affinity have experienced. There we can find the examples of pacifism and antimilitarism—one might mention the names of Tolstoy and Gandhi—of movements dedicated to contesting imperialism and racism, of those engaged in the struggle against all forms of ethnocentrism, of networks dedicated to bringing an end to the exploitation and marginalization experienced by women, of animal rights organizations, of vegetarianism and veganism, of those who have built counterculture, Situationism, and Zapatismo, of those who have decided to confront capitalist globalization, or of those who have given priority to ecological concerns and, hence, the discussion around environmental and resource limits of the planet. I am referring to movements that have been nurtured by libertarian thought—whose current state would be difficult to explain without this influence—and that, in turn, have updated its perceptions, always, as Daniel Barret recalls, from a horizon of anti-capitalism, anti-statism, and anti-authoritarianism.[12]

---

12 Daniel Barret (Rafael Spósito), *Los sediciosos despertares de la anarquía* (Buenos Aires/Montevideo: Anarres/Terramar/Nordan, 2011), 224.

The Individual and the Collective

The vast majority of the traditions of anarchist thought have in fact a *socialist* or *communist* character. Consequently, it is argued that it is in society and in social life where the greatest human virtues are revealed; namely, cooperation, solidarity, and mutual aid. It is further stated that social life has been the object of various historical aggressions, with many of them originating in the state.

As a result, it is important to remember that libertarians ultimately have always assumed a thorough defense of the individual and her powers. Despite anarchist thinkers having attributed, at times, different meanings to the word *freedom*, all of them, without exception, understand that it is a central element of any emancipatory project. It is enough to recall that for Emmanuel Mounier, dignity, rebellion, and emancipation were the three concepts that gave strength to anarchism and that referred to what is most profound in a human being.[13] From this perspective, it is furthermore necessary to assert the voluntary character of any adherence to anarchism: there is nothing more absurd than the pretension to impose libertarian communism or anything like it.

A colleague reproached me recently for including a text by Max Stirner, the individualist anarchist *par excellence*, in the anthology of libertarian thought that I submitted for publication in 2010. I believe that the criticism, though legitimate, was unjust. Stirner is not the wild and misunderstood individualist that he has been commonly portrayed to be. In

---

Many of the terms regarding the contemporary debate about anarchism are outlined in Alfredo M. Bonanno, *El anarquismo entre la teoría y la práctica* (n.p.: Bardo, 2013); Jonathan Purkis and James Bowen, eds., *Changing Anarchism: Anarchist Theory and Practice in the Global Age* (Manchester: Manchester University, 2004), and Duanes Rousselle and Süreyyya Evren, eds., *Post-anarchism: A Reader* (London: Pluto Press, 2011).

13 Édouard Jourdain, *L'anarchisme* (Paris: La Découverte, 2013), 94.

actuality, the majority of the so-called individualist anarchists do not reject forms of collective organization and action. What they do reject, as do most anarchists, are those forms of organization and action that imply, in one way or another, the use of authoritarian procedures. Thus, individualist anarchism—which is not my kind of anarchism—has contributed, for instance, to a healthy and radical challenge of all institutions—not only the state—and their corresponding relations of power. Accordingly, it has also been rewarding for the more emblematic currents of *social* anarchism. Given that not everything is reducible to the power of the state or capital and that this power can frequently take on elaborate forms quite difficult to perceive, defending the autonomy of the individual against it is always an honorable and a necessary task.

This is particularly so in light of the fact that the majority of the traditions that find their inspiration in Marx's thought barely pay any attention to the condition and defense of the individual, as they often concern themselves only with new and old forms of domination and alienation. And it remains surprising to find in Marx's epigones—and in Marx himself as well—many deficiencies concerning the different manifestations of domination.

Human Nature

How human nature is perceived in anarchist thought is an endless discussion. From the outset, we might suspect that the basis for the dispute is an easily identifiable fact: neither Godwin, Stirner, Bakunin, nor Kropotkin share the same conception. Peter Marshall, a historian of anarchism, has referred in this regard to Godwin's rational benevolence, Stirner's conscious egoism, Bakunin's destructive energy, and Kropotkin's calm altruism.[14] Apart from this, one is liable to

---

14 Peter Marshall, *Demanding the Impossible: A History of Anarchism*

find almost anything among anarchists: from ascetics and libertines, hedonists and the circumspect, to the affable and asocial, the lovers of work and defenders of the right to laziness, to the creative and the sordid.

Many of the expressions of anarchist thought seem to question the existence of a discernable human nature bearing at all times and places some kind of inexorable essence, such as the "will to power" Nietzsche spoke about or a stark bent toward competitiveness. Still, a common fact that stands out among anarchists is the conviction that the human being is capable of living, through mutual aid and solidarity, without coercion and authority. Failing this, the ascendancy of the latter two is the result of a vested operation that distorts primordial reality and demonstrates the degree to which power corrupts and generates undesirable practices and values. This is perceived in such terms to make clear, at the same time, that the suppression of power does not end these practices and values. Anarchist thought starts from the assumption that human nature modulates itself, depending on the circumstances, through various factors. Despite human nature being the product of its environment, as this environment can change, so too can human nature.

It is often said that anarchism embraces a romantic and *do-gooder* vision that consequently tends to idealize the human condition. Even though there is no shortage of arguments to support such a conclusion, there are also well-founded arguments supporting the opposite. I believe, in fact, that the rejection of power and coercive authority typical of anarchism can only be explained by a realistic fear of the consequences of such forces.

It is perhaps necessary to recall, in short, that many anarchist thinkers do not conceive of revolution as an explosive social rupture but rather as something that refers, to a considerable degree, to the recuperation of values and ways of conduct that have always been present, though often hidden. Let us not forget that, for Kropotkin, mutual aid was a common principle in stateless societies. A similar idea is expressed in the following words by German anarchist Gustav Landauer: "The State is a condition, a certain relationship between human beings, a mode of behaviour; we destroy it by contracting other relationships, by behaving differently toward one another."[15]

Without Leaders

When we argue that we need leaders, it is as if we were referring to a biological process that is natural, rational, and inexorable. Such a necessity, however, has an ideological and induced character and is but another consequence of the rules of a system intent on efficiently reproducing itself. Consequently, the rejection of leaders is not a caprice, for they quite literally exemplify the condition of the model that we suffer under.

Furthermore, an idea has often been put forth, in an apparently more cautious way, whereby leadership, though an unhealthy reality, represents an intrinsic part of the organization of human societies; thus, we would have no other choice but to accept it. This is a quite common thesis, particularly in many of the Marxist-inspired critiques of anarchism. The reply is straightforward: on the basis of an argument of this kind, one would also have to accept accordingly many of the other characteristics of our social reality, such as exploitation, alienation, or the absence of solidarity.

Although the expression *anarchist leader* is indeed a contradiction in terms, the problem of leadership has revealed itself to be—let us not forget—at the very heart of libertarian organizations. It is worth remembering the intense polemics

---

15 Gustav Landauer, quoted in Paul Avrich, *Anarchist Portraits* (Princeton: Princeton University Press, 1988), 252.

during the 1930s caused by the creation of the Federación Anarquista Ibérica (FAI—Iberian Anarchist Federation) and its real or supposed intention to control, as a self-proclaimed vanguard, the entire libertarian movement. Bakunin himself was often accused, and not without reason, of seeking to create secret and hierarchical organizations. There was, of course, another side to the Russian revolutionary, one that, in his defense, expressed a prophetic suspicion—which I already have referred to—with regard to a society governed by socialist savants which he believed was defended by Marx. And even though it seems obvious that the latter was not always an authoritarian and vanguardist Jacobin, this ideological trait was very present in his work and particularly in his conduct.

That this problem did indeed exist does not mean there were no records of significant responses to it. In many of the publications of Spanish anarchism, there was a predomination of articles, generally anonymous, by persons of humble origin. In addition, it was frequently debated whether it was convenient to identify the authors of such collaborations, in an evident desire to contest leadership and personalism.[16] It seems, furthermore, as if the potential leaders that anarchist movements had embraced did not possess the same kind of characteristics that shaped this phenomenon in other scenarios. They referred more to intellectual and moral qualities— even if, through those, the discussion could arise in more traditional terms—than to the status of individuals who exercised a power that was beyond control.

I should add that, in the case of the anarchist movements, as I have had already noted, there was no strict doctrine to administer and supervise. The movement saw itself as collective and, as a result, susceptible of self-correction. Therefore, there was no place for self-proclaimed vanguards from within, bearers of a supposedly superior knowledge, who so often

---

16 Édouard Waintrop, *Les anarchists espagnols, 1968–1981* (Denoël, 2012), 93–94.

revealed themselves to be behind those they claimed to be leading. As the Russian anarchist Voline said:

> The key idea of anarchism is simple: no party, or political or ideological group, even if it sincerely desires to do so, will ever succeed in emancipating the working masses by placing itself above or outside them in order to "govern" or "guide" them. True emancipation can only be brought about by the direct action...of those concerned, the workers themselves, through their own class organizations (production syndicates, factory committees, cooperatives, etc.) and not under the banner of any political party or ideological body. Their emancipation must be based on concrete action and "self-administration," aided but not controlled by revolutionaries working from within the masses and not from above them.[17]

It is not inappropriate to follow the intuition that, instead of underscoring the proud rejection of leaders, what is worth stressing here is that which replaces them; that is to say, the direct democracy of equals.

Utopia

Many of the criticisms leveled against libertarian thought do not refer to the general meaning of the project it defends, but rather, and more precisely, to its viability. Quite frequently, a special focus is placed on its presumably *utopian* nature, far removed from the real possibilities that—so we are told—human societies offer.

The first response to this argument takes the form of a frank advocacy of utopia. This—say the libertarians—does not have a negative character, which is what Marx and Engels

---

17 Voline, in Daniel Guérin, *Anarchism: From Theory to Practice*, trans. Mary Koppler (New York: Monthly Review Press, 1970), 37–38.

attributed, for instance, to the *utopian* socialists. Delving deeper, Peter Marshall states sensibly that anarchism is utopian in that it permanently imagines a world that may be, but it is at the same time very realistic to the extent that its foundations rest upon deeply rooted traditions of mutual aid.[18] Anarchists are, in addition, very realistic, both in regard to the assessment of the existing order as well as to the proposal of the unavoidable need for a new one, for which they have outlined thorough programs based on a combination of collective action and respect for personal autonomy. As a result, they seem to deliver suggestive responses to the problems of the society of our time; responses, however, that do not partake of worldviews boasting their allegedly realistic characters. If libertarian thought displays, on the one hand, an unparalleled pessimism in regard to power, it also manifests, on the other, a notable optimism concerning the possibility of reestablishing human relations marked by codes of equality and solidarity.

Nevertheless, we must admit that it is difficult to put anarchist ideas into practice. What would we gain, however, if we renounced the attempt, especially when there are ever more people who do not perceive in them—and this instills fear in those who govern us—a distant and incomprehensible endeavor? And does anyone seriously believe, in short, that anarchism, with its conception of the relation between means and ends, is any more utopian than social democracy or Leninism? A nineteenth-century French anarchist song provides an ironic answer to many of our difficulties: after proclaiming that capitalism has been abolished, a daring question is placed in the mouth of one of its protagonists— who will now pay for the Saturday newspaper?—to which the answer is simple, once capitalism and its rules have been thrown into the dustbin of history.

---

18 Marshall, *Demanding the Impossible*, 705.

II.

DELEGATIVE DEMOCRACY, DIRECT DEMOCRACY

A Critique of Democracy

ALTHOUGH ADVOCACY FOR direct democracy is a common trait of libertarian thought, there are in fact more and more people who seem to conclude that, given the general degradation in the very use of the word *democracy*, the moment has arrived to seek less worn-out terms. While many libertarian thinkers distinguish among forms of political power based on their degree of perversion, they try not to delude themselves about the essential meaning of liberal democracy. And when referring to the latter, one often speaks of farce and exploitation, of inequality and injustice, of the illusion of representation, and of the manipulation by the media at the service of power.

27

The libertarian critique of liberal democracy suggests that, despite the rhetoric, it has nothing to do with the celebrated principle of majority rule: it is rather based on ruling minorities who coercively generate self-interested consensuses and repress everything that works against these consensuses. It seems curious that the principle of "one man, one vote" is applied to underpin a system that rests on a scientific and unchangeable organization of inequality that, yes, makes use of an apparent plurality developed within a closed circuit. Lastly, liberal democracy seems inexorably linked to the activity of a parasitic human group. As Bakunin argued, "the representative system, far from being a guarantee for the people, on the contrary, creates and safeguards the continued existence of a governmental aristocracy against the people."[1]

We should also ask ourselves why liberal democracy manifestly leaves the economy and the world of work outside its purview or, even worse, subordinates the political system to the interests of powerful private companies. From a project that serves the visible purpose of ratifying the privileges of the powerful, the majority is paradoxically excluded from the making of decisions. Just as economic power concentrates itself, the same occurs with political power, in a scenario weighed down by oligarchy and inequality. Liberal democracy, in sum, brings in its wake a general aggression against all kinds of alternative, horizontal, and egalitarian organizations. As a result, it clearly negates diversity and endeavors to completely cancel out the possibility of searching for other horizons.

I will therefore underline the fact that the farce of democracy evidently has perfected itself, for it no longer displays the same characteristics that it did in the days of Bakunin or Kropotkin. It has greased the mechanisms of integration offered by the illusions of consumption, the generation of dependencies, or the recognition of fictional rights. It is easy to

---

1   Mikhail Bakunin, quoted in Guérin, *Anarchism*, 17.

see, however, a recent and irrepressible authoritarian shift and a directed effort, not without paradox, to cancel or mitigate the influence of the aforementioned mechanisms of integration. The disaster of the current political scenario is not the result of a random shift; it inevitably arises from the foundations of liberal democracy and was perhaps unavoidable. Whoever believes at this point that corruption is a problem linked to certain persons or circumstances, I am afraid, fails to grasp what is fundamentally at stake.

Elections

Elections lie at the heart of liberal democracy. I am still fascinated by the reverberations that elections continue to have in the minds of so many people. Whoever puts forth a different prospect must painstakingly justify their options, whereas the huge flaws of the electoral path go unnoticed. The most problematic elements impose themselves in an extremely effective way when the logic to which the elections correspond is interiorized as normal and democratic: there is no better way to control people and annihilate dissent. Even more surprising, in particular, is the fascination that elections inspire among many *leftists*, who appear to believe blindly in them. It is noteworthy, though, that one no longer hears a shameful argument that used to have some following in the past, one that called the attention to the possibility of using elections and parliaments as platforms for the dissemination of ideas.

As elections imply leaving everything in the hands of others who will resolve our problems in the future and—one must assume—liberate us, the mythical belief in them is a sign of desperation and an abandonment of action. This situation is all the more significant in the case of libertarians, since the critique of elections rests on solidly established, preconceived grounds—above all, one that involves a permanent refusal of delegation—and on a simple and empirical reflection on contemporary reality. It is worth recalling that elections convene the pre-existing bewilderment and igno-rance of the population, which is usually completely unaware of the political programs of the parties for which they vote; and they are a dubious representation of the will of the ma-jority, to the extent that the victorious parties—with internal structures that are anything but democratic—obtain modest percentages of the vote, especially when abstention is tak-en into account. Elections also reflect dramatic differences in the resources available to those political parties and all the common injustices of electoral systems. As I have men-tioned above, the economy is left almost exclusively on the sidelines of parliamentary decisions, while the judiciary col-laborates actively and without any independence whatsoever in the general plot; we also hear, more and more frequently in speeches and in the miscommunication media, techno-cratic discourses suggesting that our main problems are not *political* but rather merely technical. And should anything fail, there await states of exception and coups d'état waiting in the wings, accompanied by a the ever-present prospect of repression. Where then is popular sovereignty? The voters are the extras who work for free in a farcical film, the film of de-mocracy, in which "freedom is reduced to a choice between brands of detergent in the aisles of a shopping center."[2]

In this scenario, a critique of libertarian practices (a cri-tique of electoral abstention), which has often been expressed from the trenches of organizations and by people who claim Marx's thought, cannot but be surprising. This critique states that, by not participating in elections and institutions, lib-ertarians leave the path open for the forces of capital to take over,[3] as if there were not already enough consistent and con-stant examples of the uselessness of elections and institutions

---

2   Various Authors, *Materiales para una crítica de la democracia* (Madrid: Klinamen, 2009), 7.

3   For an example of this kind of combat literature, see John Molyneux, *Anarchism: A Marxist Criticism* (London: Bookmarks, 2011).

and of the capacity that liberal democracy demonstrates when it comes to co-opting those who decide to abide by its rules. This double conclusion—that this apparent democracy paves the way, without any caveats, to possible rupture and that it can't prevent damage to the edifice of capitalism—can only be described as naive: "If voting changed anything, they'd make it illegal," proclaims a well-known slogan. A more sensible conclusion would be that the overwhelming majority of advances secured by workers have had little or nothing to do with elections. In fact, the general crisis of reformist unionism bears an obvious relation to the precedence given to it, responsible for draining the blood out of many of the organizations of struggle of days past. Is it even feasible to emancipate the people from above, from the institutions, and get them to do what in other circumstances they would never do?

In the libertarian world, the question of elections has certainly provoked more or less intense debates. Here I am not referring to the ontological discussion around the ballot box: it is clear that exercising the right to vote in groups of voluntary membership is not the same as voting in elections regulated by self-interested institutions. Nevertheless, and in regard to those regulated elections, there are some who deem it necessary to proudly and publicly advocate for abstention, whereas others believe that they should simply be forgotten. Those who position themselves within this second alternative put forward the argument that to call for abstention is in fact to attribute to elections an importance that they do not deserve and, in a certain way, to participate in them. Ricardo Mella, considered to be the main Spanish anarchist theorist, proposes a third path of action, one that suggests respect for the decision to vote but that also stresses the necessity of turning the weight of our attention to everyday direct action, which is far more important and effective.[4]

---

4   Ricardo Mella, "Vota, pero escucha," in *Solidaridad Obrera*, December 25, 1909.

Direct Democracy

I have stated above that the word *democracy* is so worn out that one might just as well seek a different one to capture its corresponding referents. Something similar occurs with the term *transition*: reference to it originated in the second half of the 1970s and is so shameful that there are more than enough motives to suspect the good sense of the defense of a *second transition*.[5]

The truth is, despite all this, there exists a clear defense of direct democracy in the libertarian world. This defense rests on a rejection of delegation and representation, the proposal of organizations with neither coercion nor leaders, and the repudiation of any type of government. To be feasible, all of the above logically demands a prior and active process of decentralization, decomplexification, and a reduction of the size of political communities. The logic of direct democracy leads inevitably to a contestation of the world of political parties, which is none other than the world of delegation and separation, of leaders and hierarchies, of elections and parliaments. The organizational and party-oriented wager of the *traditional left* is not only challenged by the libertarian response: it must also face the seemingly nebulous and anomic condition of many of the emergent networks.

Over the last few years, the discussion around direct democracy has brought about the development of an interesting and polemical new concept connected with so-called libertarian municipalism. Although the idea has various expressions, I will limit myself to mentioning the many libertarians who seem to approve of the participation in local

---

5   Taibo is referring, first, to Spain's transition from dictatorship under Francisco Franco to a form of liberal democracy—a transition that was controlled and shaped by the outgoing authoritarian regime. The term *second transition* has been used more recently to describe contemporary changes in Spanish democracy that render it, allegedly, more sophisticated than its earlier forms. [editor]

elections where, at least on paper, it is possible to maintain many of the characteristic elements of direct democracy, thereby limiting the exercise of representation to a significant degree. This was, in sum, the project embraced initially by the Candidatura d'Unitat Popular (CUP—Popular Unity Candidacy) in Catalonia. In no way do I wish to settle the debate on libertarian municipalism or to categorically reject the possible virtues of this proposal. But I am obliged to express my fears, which are essentially three. The first emphasizes that libertarian municipalism presupposes the acceptance of a category that has a clear institutional dimension. As such, it carries with it the evident risk of co-option, especially when the project implies assuming the rules of the political game imposed by the system (even if this is often accompanied, indeed, by the ambition of changing these very rules). The second of these fears takes the form of a question (and here I refer again to the model of the Catalan CUP in its more recent incarnation, which may result in more traditional forms like those identified with Sortu [in the Basque Country] or Syriza [in Greece]). Is it not rather easy to imagine that the project under consideration may lead, in a headlong rush, to a compliance with situations unequivocally governed by delegation and representation? The third caveat reminds us that libertarian municipalism today does not seem to provide any tangible benefits that have not been offered before by the noninstitutional practice of direct democracy.

I would like to add that the debate about direct democracy has always been marked by complaints regarding the supposed impossibility of realizing it. Thus, Leninists, social democrats, and liberal-conservatives have often found a common voice, without ever asking themselves about the suitability of their models and without reflecting on the extent to which the hostility that they bestow on direct democracy does not even constitute a partial explanation of many of its manifestations' possible failure. Beyond this, I suspect that the insistence of these three political currents is not about underscoring the difficulties associated with the application of direct democracy in complex societies but rather about defending the advantages that representative pseudo-democracy has for the existing disorder. In such a scenario, I will only state my belief that the system we suffer under is perfectly well prepared to confront the very relative oppositional spasms that Leninists and social democrats brandish, while it is less able, however, to respond to the challenge of democracy from below.

Direct Action

We often forget that direct democracy has an inevitable correlate in libertarian thought, one that calls for direct action. Graeber has asserted in this regard that while Marxism tends to be a theoretical or analytical reflection on revolutionary strategy, anarchism rather signifies an ethical discourse about revolutionary practice.[6]

By *direct action* I mean the kind of action in which we are active participants, without external mediations—political parties, bureaucracies, governments—and that is aimed at the self-managed control of life itself, in such a way that we retain fully and at every moment the capacity to decide on it. The corresponding proposal advocates self-organization at the margins of institutions, demands avoiding intermediaries and outside instructions, and, in the majority of cases, advises the circumvention of any demand of, or negotiation with, whomever exercises power. The latter dimension has certainly divided a movement like that of 15-M for quite some time, in that one of its components essentially advances the elaboration of proposals, trusting that these will be heard by those who govern, while another aspires to open spaces of autonomy, self-management, and decommodification

---

6   David Graeber, *Direct Action: An Ethnography* (AK Press: Oakland, 2009), 211.

without waiting for any authorization from any governing leaders.

Direct action is also born out of a desire to control, in an unmediated way, the events that follow from it. We seek to act as if we were free because, in so doing, we begin to be so. In this sense, it additionally possesses a prefigurative character, to the extent that it is based on the idea that means and ends should be in concordance with each other. "Beware of the present you create, for it should resemble the future that you dream of," reads a slogan of Mujeres Creando, a Bolivian anarcho-feminist collective of street agitators. The prefigurative condition that I have just mentioned is a trait that is obviously absent, by contrast, from civil disobedience.[7] After all, the latter unequivocally accepts the existing order, to the extent that it demands simply the right to disobey any law that it considers unjust. But how can civil disobedience be managed at all when it is understood that the majority of the laws, if not all of them, are unjust?

I will add that direct action maintains a close relation to what for more than a hundred years was commonly called *propaganda by the deed*, in the sense that the latter almost always had a more ambitious condition and, more often than not, was linked to an insurrection that was to become in itself the basis for many others. Still, the connection between direct action and propaganda by the deed necessarily leads to the conclusion that the first cannot remain a mere symbolic or aesthetic action; rather, it must lead to tangible, material changes on the ground.

---

7   Benjamin Franks, in Robert Graham (ed.), *Anarchism: A Documentary History of Libertarian Ideas, Volume 3: The New Anarchism (1974–2012)* (Montreal: Black Rose Books, 2013), 86.

III.

THE STATE

Insisting on the State

It is widely known that anarchists consider the state as a major enemy. The corresponding perception is born out of a certainty: as Proudhon often rightly pointed out, the state is in no way a natural and neutral power that imparts justice and protects the weak. The idea that the state protects us has been encouraged with singular enthusiasm in the last decades by two moribund projects: that of social democracy and reformist syndicalism. And it is a cause for concern that those who claim to contest capitalism take on this idea uncritically, without submitting the matter to any discussion whatsoever.

The state is not an autonomous institution that lives outside capital, as even some anarchists have been prone to believe. Because of this, the aim of controlling and governing capital to bring an end to it is meaningless, sometimes because the project is mired in the miseries of social democracy, other times because it simply becomes a sterile exercise. The corresponding optical illusions, however, perfectly illustrate the undeniable success attained by the systems we suffer under at generating artificial and self-interested consensuses and at the parallel task of brutally centralizing power.

However, if the state's significance seems clear in capitalism, it is no less so when this institution is at the service of a supposedly *socialist* project: the Soviet experience, which felt like *bureaucratic state capitalism* on the ground, categorically demonstrated that the state that was forged under its aegis subordinated itself to the interests of a new dominant class. Though the idea that a transition phase is necessary to move from capitalism to socialism—or to whatever—seems as reasonable as it is respectable, in no way does this oblige us to accept that the state must be an inevitable step toward such a transition. Likewise, it is important to remember that, despite the majority of the variations of the options *reform* and *revolution* having unfortunately interpreted the state as the main transforming agent, the credibility of the state for each has forcibly, and notably, weakened over the course of the last hundred years.

John Holloway has stated that the principal error of revolutionary movements of a Marxist character has not been to deny the capitalist nature of the state but rather to have misunderstood the degree to which it is integrated in capitalist social relations. Holloway has himself indicated that the notion that society can be changed by means of the state rests on the idea that the state is sovereign, in such a way that the struggle for social change transforms itself into a struggle for the defense of state sovereignty. "The struggle against capital then becomes an anti-imperialist struggle against domination by foreigners, in which nationalism and anti-capitalism are blended."[1] Thus, argues Holloway, self-determination and state sovereignty are confused, whereas the essence of the state is completely antithetical to the perspective of

---

1   John Holloway, *Change the World without Taking Power* (New York: Pluto Press, 2010), 16.

self-determination (or that of self-management, I would add). Holloway concludes, then, that Leninism is based on a formidable equivocation, which suggests that the concept of state power is the culmination of the drive toward self-determination—a drive that, in the Russian case, was born in the soviets.[2]

Yet we must also pay attention to another central aspect of the state, its repressive condition—armies, police, prisons, mental institutions, schools, media—which has always been much more relevant than its welfare-protective side. Who protects us from the state? Repression and war are inherent to it—a process that has been ratified in recent times—in direct opposition to the sustained illusions of the recent past. A relatively new phenomenon has been gaining ground as well, a hyper-controlling design. The intrinsically coercive nature of the state is based, as David Graeber has repeatedly suggested, on a fundamental contradiction: when it claims for itself a monopoly on the use of violence, it grounds this pretention on a power that is distinct from it; that is, on acts that were considered illegal under the judicial system prior to that of the state itself, which in turn arises as a result of violent acts that were considered illegal at the time when they were committed.[3] Graeber emphasizes how the French revolutionaries of 1789 were guilty of high treason from the perspective of the order they were engaged in contesting. If the kings, who self-interestedly positioned themselves at the margins of this order, found in such an operation an arrangement to free themselves from their own predicament, the same cannot be said, however, about "the people." The latter are invoked as the legitimizing source of state violence whenever, in panic, the possibility of a genuine democratization of the regulating

---

2   Ibid., 232.

3   David Graeber, "There Never Was a West, or Democracy Emerges from the Spaces in Between," in *Possibilities: Essays on Hierarchy, Rebellion, and Desire* (Oakland: AK Press, 2007), 366.

legal procedures is considered. The people are therefore a merely rhetorical, but never material, foundation of the order of state violence, which is always unbridled and completely escapes popular direction and control on the ground. In such conditions, the libertarian option gains weight due to its strict rationality, asserting that the revolution can in no way be carried out through the coercive power of the state; rather, it must be grounded on social organization from the grassroots.

It is, of course, true that many of the features of the institution of the state have continued to change over time. For instance, the typical Western European, nineteenth-century state—with its appended electoral farces and absence of welfare concerns—equipped itself in the twentieth century with a patina of *democracy* seasoned with apparent links to the *well-being* of the population. As I will suggest later on, it seems we are obliged to free ourselves from the many mirages that have surrounded the *social state under the rule of law*. The authoritarian shift of the institution of the state and its utter submission to private interests, ever more evident of late, only strengthen the anarchist diagnosis, seemingly undermined by welfare states. Lastly, to summarize the argument underlining the fact that, over the course of the last centuries, numerous parasites have made the state their home, one may add with certainty that today we speak of a machine that also lives at the expense of future generations. Is it possible, perhaps, that the state of the future will fully realize Arthur Koestler's old adage that in a totalitarian state, everything that is not forbidden is compulsory?

Welfare States

From a libertarian perspective, the formulation of a general critique of what welfare states have presupposed in the second half of the twentieth century in Western Europe (there are no manifestations of this phenomenon outside of this geographical area) is inevitable. With this end in mind, it must be noted that welfare states are institutions inherent to, and exclusively of, capitalism. We must also emphasize that they carry with them mechanisms for the delegation of power and for making decisions over resources that escape any logic of self-management and popular control, always placing the state at the center of all processes. We can attest to their clear relation to a dead project, that of social democracy, calling attention to their links to forms of submissive reformist unionism, of the kind endorsed by our Comisiones Obreras (CC. OO.—Workers' Commissions) and the Unión General de Trabajadores (UGT—General Union of Workers). We may also note their unequivocal and, to a certain degree, paradoxical relation with a care economy whose negative burden falls overwhelmingly on women and raises profound doubts about its ecological sustainability. It is worth remembering also that these institutions are modes of economic and social organization characteristic of countries of the global North, lacking any indication of a desire for solidarity with the inhabitants of the global South. In short, we touch a raw nerve on what is most problematic—namely, the welfare states' evident aim of pacifying open challenges to the system that we suffer under.

Once this critique is presented, an anything-but-insignificant problem comes into view: if, on the one hand, it would be unwise to dismiss what we are told, on the other hand, the logical demands made by people in regard to health, education, or retirement pensions ought to be attended to accordingly. We cannot say to an elderly person, for example, that, since we are engaged in the creation of an ambitious program of libertarian communes, she should renounce her pension and the primary healthcare provided by social security. The main response that has been formulated to this problem has consisted of a defense of *self-managed* and *socialized* public health and education. Though this response implies a laudable awareness that the problem exists, we must admit that it does not resolve the matter completely. And there is a reason for all this that is easy to identify: the logic of self-management and socialization fits very poorly—doesn't fit, in actuality—with that of the state, and this gives rise to insurmountable contradictions.

Nevertheless, I will try to discuss the matter in more practical terms. Today the demands for the preservation of the welfare state clash against two fundamental obstacles. The first has to do with what may be seen as an unfortunate mirage: that it would be possible for us to return to 2007, to the situation prior to the eruption of the *financial crisis*, in utter ignorance—that is why I speak of a mirage—of the fact that what we have today is a direct result of what we had back then. But this aside, it is inevitable to conclude that, from a libertarian perspective, the majority of people demand more than a simple reconstruction of a supposedly regulated capitalism. The second obstacle is born out of an inexorable question: how much time do we devote to setting matters right in the fields of health, education, or pensions, given that the reconstruction of the welfare state calls for the participation of political parties, parliaments, and institutions that do not appear to be up to the task or, to state things more correctly, that endorse privatizations and budget cuts with or without impertinence? If we assume a response that does not go beyond what political parties, parliaments, and institutions can contribute, shall we not find ourselves condemned to accept a scenario by virtue of which the welfare state will be, despite the good intentions of some, even more rickety in the services proffered than it has always been and will thereby contribute to increasing the burdens already mentioned above?

I have many times spoken about how years ago, in the heat of one of the many student demonstrations, I got used to reciting the litany that advocated for a public, universal, free, secular, and qualitative education. One day, as I enunciated it, I recalled that decades before, when I was a university student, we used to harshly criticize state public education because we understood it as a central mechanism for the reproduction of the logic of capital. And we were not off track: far from any prospect of self-management, public education has often promoted compliance with authority, obedience, unrestrained competition, individualism, the primacy of values of the ruling classes, and submission before the reigning order. What happened during the passage of those years? The regression that we experienced in every domain prompted many to dig trenches and to come out in defense of public education to avoid even greater evils. However logically forgivable this decision was in itself, it will be quite unfortunate, though, if it turns into an incentive to reproduce once more the logic of capital. If—let us repeat—the words *self-management* and *socialization* impose themselves as antidotes, it will be good to be aware that they fit very, very poorly with the state as institution. It would certainly be even worse should *private* anarchist schools respond, as it frequently happens with some of them, with elitist projects far removed from the grassroots.

Where the State Ends

The discussion regarding welfare states—a term that gratuitously embellishes the corresponding reality—takes place on an uncertain terrain, configured by concepts that are not always useful inasmuch as they are understood by everyone in different ways. The public sphere, for example, does not necessarily pertain to the state, even though the identification of the two realities has gained such weight that it is difficult to separate them. Alternately, the private sphere does not refer ontologically to individualisms and egoisms: from a justifiable perspective, an anarchist school has a *private* character. I will close this brief exposé of equivocations with the reminder that it is ever more frequent for the public sphere to be linked with what is *common*, in an approach in which apparently the terms *self-management* and *socialization* fit smoothly. Finally

I would add that the problems are not often resolved, or they are resolved too conveniently, given that the state categorically refuse to do so, becuase it is inclined to forget delicate situations and complex issues. Consider the following example: standing in solidarity with a people expelled from their land in Galilee or in the Negev and locked in a jail in Gaza and the West Bank, I shall confess that, although I never sympathized with the proposal to create an eventual Palestinian state, I would like to be sensible enough to acknowledge that such a proposal does not come out of thin air and that it rather aims at the resolution of urgent problems, certainly at the expense, no doubt, of creating new ones.

Whatever the facts, the temptation to objectify the state and aggrandize it excessively is occasionally evident in anarchist thought, as if it were the only enemy and the only source of power. In the same way that many Marxist thinkers have been obsessed with relations of production, many anarchists have behaved similarly toward the state. One of the consequences of this exercise in objectification and aggrandizement that calls itself to my attention may very well be that the other manifestations of power, more or less autonomous with respect to the state, are left to oblivion. There is a kind of anarchism that identifies the latter exclusively with ministries—the revolution would have to be carried out with picks and shovels and violence—and fails to consider that we carry power and its rules in our heads, afflicted as we are by very different kinds of oppression. If we situate the state within the general framework of oppressions, its image dissipates—there is something more than the state—while it strengthens itself, whenever it lies unequivocally at the center of these oppressions.

There are also expressions of libertarian discourse that—and I will come back to this—obsessed with the state, leave capitalism in the background or pay no attention to preceding phenomena, such as patriarchal society. Let us not forget that certain currents of libertarian thought, like anarcho-primitivism, seem to argue that the main cause of our ills and problems is not the state but rather something prior to it that sustains it: the very human civilization we are familiar with. From this vantage point, to content ourselves with a critique of the state would often mean to contest what is superficial and elude what lies within.

IV.

CAPITALISM, CLASS STRUGGLE, SELF-MANAGEMENT

Anti-Capitalism

I HAVE ALREADY noted that a large part of the ills we suffer are certainly a product of capitalism, even if all of them were not created by it. It would hardly be surprising then that anarchism, which is, for better or worse, contemporaneous with the industrial capitalism of the nineteenth century, in its doctrinal dimension has always assumed an inevitable clash with capital and its interests. It seems a relatively simple task to determine what anarchist theorists consider inherent to capitalism: exclusion and exploitation, inequality and marginalization, and, above all, the order of private property. Faced with such a pernicious social system, which may nevertheless be individually gratifying, collectivist and communist anarchists—that is to say, the majority of them—advocate first for the expropriation and then the socialization of property in the framework of a revolution commonly referred to as *social*, and not merely *political*. We should remember that, when the libertarians of Aragon of the 1930s declared libertarian communism in their villages and towns, the first thing they did was burn the property records.

Furthermore, libertarian thought argues that there exists no possibility of autonomy and self-management whatsoever under capitalism, which logically implies exiting from it. To do so, therefore, does not necessarily mean calling for any deterministic schema as proposed by the *mature* Marx, nor does it urgently require the existence of any particular elements. Landauer stated in this respect, "I have repeated on many occasions that socialism is possible and necessary regardless of the economy or technology; it is not linked to the large industry of the global market, and has little need of the industrial and commercial technology of capitalism."[1] In conformity with this perspective, history is built on the basis of a combination of conditions and will, but the former do not establish anything firm, inevitable, or indubitable.

Class Struggle

The dispute over capitalism is, in one of its principal dimensions, the dispute over class struggle. Today, when class struggle led by better-off workers [*los de arriba*] has attained particular notoriety, a reflection imposes itself on the kind of struggle those from below engage or ought to engage in. And it imposes itself because class struggle has often become an icon whose meaning gives rise to little more than disagreements and differences.

The first reflection in this regard must inevitably be about the *working class*. I must confess that I am equally suspicious of those who believe that the working class has diluted itself

---

1 Gustav Landauer, quoted in Offensive, *Construire l'autonomie. Se réapproprier le travail, le commerce, la ruralité* (Montreuil: L'Echappée, 2012), 177.

into nothingness—stating that it is an artifact of the past—and those who fail to discern any relevant changes in its condition. If the first of these attitudes usually ends in a vague citizenist [*ciudadanista*] impulse, the second usually translates into the sterile repetition of old slogans and nonsense. In the last decades, we have witnessed a certain decomposition of the traditional classes, which have produced distinct manifestations often in tension with each other. The phenomenon is quite clear in the case of the working class, fragmented by various factors, such as unemployment, precariousness, underemployment, part-time employment, and the weight of the underground economy. In virtue of a parallel process, there are many experts who identify in the traditional working class, or in what remains of it, a position of relative privilege responsible for conservative conduct, which push the working class into a confrontation between subproletarians and lumpenproletarians who are increasingly punished. Notwithstanding the above, there are also those who see a distinction between the *laboring class* and the *working class*. But who would fall within the first of these categories, the more general of the two? As Holloway argues, would Marx and Engels, the rebels of Chiapas, feminists, those active in the gay movement, the police, belong to this category?[2] Is it useful, in the end, to reduce the laboring class to the urban proletariat that works in factories, knowing full well that it is an increasingly less numerous human group?

If we assume, and there is probably little choice but to do so, that the working class is no longer the unquestionable subject that suffers exploitation or that leads the struggle for emancipation, it would nevertheless be a mistake to forget that, despite it all, it is still there. How could we abandon the contestation in the working world? When we speak of self-management, the first thing that comes to mind is, logically and inevitably, factories and companies (and certainly

---

2   Holloway, *Change the World without Taking Power*, 141.

other instances as well). The existence of problems related to the revolutionary subject's condition cannot be interpreted as forgetting what the working class presupposes; likewise, it cannot justify the conclusion that we should pay no attention to what is happening to those who are declassed, lumpenized, or made precarious.

Libertarian thought has historically outlined a certain degree of preparation for the broadening of perspectives demanded by any serious reflection on the terms of contemporary class struggle. I would like to stress that Marx believed *primitive societies* and their contemporary consequences—peasants, for example—referred to a social evolution that was already over and thus could not play an active role in the awaited revolution. This perception is not shared by the majority of anarchist thinkers, who see in the peasantry in particular an attachment to the land and a laudable capacity for cooperation and mutual aid. Behind this controversy a well-known fact is revealed: if Marx seems to have believed in the proletariat as a unique revolutionary subject because he simultaneously believed in big industry, in technological development, and in what cities represented, his anarchist contemporaries—besides questioning the virtues of all these elements—embraced a more complex reality in which segments of the middle classes, peasants, and the lumpenproletariat participated, an amalgam in which one could also find not only the proletarians but also those most heavily abused.

I shall also add that this by no means suggests that nineteenth-century anarchist thinkers failed to heed the revolutionary potential of the proletariat. The distorting and reductionist vision of anarchism as a movement of artisans and petit bourgeois with a hardly—or very easily—identifiable class position must be contested. Not even the work of Proudhon, which is the lure most often used to justify this vision, reflects this claim in a convincing way. What these thinkers do—I insist—is to assess the revolutionary potential of other human groups, and not only of the proletariat. And the argument most often expressed in this regard is the one referring to the very significant role played by the peasantry in the revolutionary processes of the last century and a half already mentioned above—as is the case with the agrarian rebellions that took place in many colonized countries—despite being disqualified by Marx, who was always determined to depict peasants as idiots and reactionaries. Jean Giono pointed out, for instance, that Stalin had lowered the peasants' condition so as to make workers out of them, in lieu of raising the workers' condition in order to turn them into natural men, like the peasants.[3] Similarly, there is no sound basis to accept the Marxist disqualification of the lumpenproletariat, commonly described by the German thinker as a mere collection of antisocial elements. And Marx does not seem to have gotten matters right either in his prediction of the changes and conduct of the proletariat itself. There are many examples illustrating how some of the longer and more militant working-class struggles ultimately depend on the fact that their protagonists keep a part of their general lives, and their economic life, in the neighboring countryside, in a scenario where the boundaries between the urban and the rural blur. Murray Bookchin suggested in his writings that it was easy to discern among many of the first proletarians the healthy influence of the pre-capitalist and peasant world from which they emerged.[4]

Citizenism

It is not an easy task to explain this thing called *citizenism*, a concept that perhaps can be grasped in different ways. The first underlines its opposition to what, rightly or wrongly, has often been called *workerism* ("obrerismo"). Citizenism sets forth a series of rights that would benefit all citizens in

---

3   Offensive, *Construire l'autonomie*, 30.

4   Ibid., 203.

general, in such a way that any element linked to class struggle would find it difficult to accommodate itself to the pertinent project. In essence, it would be a proposal articulated by people clearly integrated into the logic of the system, and, as such, they would aspire to little more than a civilized management of it. A second description, closely associated with the first, considers that citizenism, content with questioning some particular elements of the reality that we endure, would fundamentally oppose itself to any sincere contestation of the system as a whole.

How has the question of citizenism manifested itself in many of the (broadly understood) contemporary *social movements*? I must first note that we may find among them those who exhibit a clear citizenist frame of reference and, by contrast, those who distance themselves from it. There are also many organizations in which co-exists often in a conflictive manner, people who position themselves within citizenism and others who do so in active opposition to the system. To describe social movements as a reality captivated by citizenism is therefore as equivocal as making them examples ontologically committed to radical contestation.

Second, I shall also note that behind the many debates there follows the dispute related to class struggle mentioned above. Whoever believes in this dispute as a central element for the articulation of emancipatory projects cannot close their eyes to—and here I am repeating arguments already proposed—the significant changes registered in the scenarios inherited from the past. The main argument reminds us that many of the characteristics that strengthened the traditional working class have been diluted, since many of those who belong to this class, with reformist labor unionism as an active collaborator, have meekly accepted the rules of the system. New issues and subjects have also appeared or consolidated themselves—the natural environment and women, to cite but two examples—forcing a rethinking of strategies and tactics, which do not necessarily call for a citizenist proposal;

some of the most profound contestations to contemporary capitalism have come precisely from feminism and ecology. Thus, it would be as problematic to forget these issues and subjects as it would be to throw the ever-present legacy of workers' struggles overboard, an option all the more disturbing when we consider the reemergence of many of the characteristics of past class struggles.

On a third level, we find the debate over *material* and *post-material* struggles. Without the least intention to provide a canonical definition, I will assert that the first refer to labor, salaried, and social relations, and they fit into what should be understood as *basic necessities*—although the matter is more complicated than it appears to be. The second, however, have emerged once these necessities were met and respond to the aim of convincingly satisfying our demands in regard to, for instance, leisure or culture. It has often been said that the anti-globalization movements of the wealthy global North situated themselves on a post-material realm, even when the movements of the global South remained, by contrast, in a material realm. Truth be told, we should ask ourselves whether this distinction, which would place citizenism in a position close to that of the post-material, has any significance whatsoever nowadays. In which of the two realms would we place, for example, ecological struggles?

Given the difficulties all of these concepts carry—we can neither do without them nor employ them without any initial critical evaluation—it seems like a simple matter to push for what ought to be the main task of those who aspire to contest capitalism as a whole: to bring together the demands of the radical working-class movement—those that come mainly, for us, from the anarcho-syndicalist world— and those emanating from non-citizenist social movements, particularly those related to women and their subjugation and exploitation, to future generations and their rights, and to many of the inhabitants of the global South. The task at hand nonetheless calls for something more: a clear challenge to the logic of states and a parallel defense—as is so often advocated in this book—of direct democracy, assemblies, self-management, and decommodification.

I believe that many of the popular assemblies of the 15-M movement, with their aim of committing themselves to the creation of autonomous spaces, self-managed and decommodified, offer a proper example of what it means to leave mere citizenist contestation behind. The everyday practice I'm concerned with here outlines, furthermore, an adequate antidote to a certain verbal radicalism that, without breaking a single dish, utters violent criticisms of the system and simultaneously scorns daily struggles, as if these were insufficiently stimulating and offered no contribution to shaping the future. If we abandon the head-on opposition to evictions or describe integral cooperatives as partial and *sell-out* projects, then it is likely the enemy will feel comforted. Likewise, a refusal of open opposition to the reality that we live under would be just as bad.

Anarcho-Syndicalism

Anarcho-syndicalism has doubtless been, particularly during the first third of the twentieth century, the principal response of the libertarian movement in the realm of labor. It is a known fact that it retains an unequalled vigor among us, however far it may be from the levels reached three quarters of a century ago.

It would seem unwise to disregard the important contribution of anarcho-syndicalism, particularly in the present moment, just as it would be foolhardy to abandon—as I have already mentioned—the world of labor. This is ever more certain when, by many measures, we seem to be returning to nineteen-century labor conditions—a circumstance that by itself calls for the reemergence of combative labor unions. Strikingly, many of the old debates thought to have been definitively discarded begin to reappear, as is the case of the one that pitted Marx against the nascent Social Democratic Party of Germany regarding capitalism's alleged inherent polarization of classes and its degradation of workers' conditions.

Unless proven otherwise, anarcho-syndicalism—as well as other formulas more or less akin to it—continues to be, its flaws notwithstanding, the primary instrument for the expression of anti-capitalist will in the libertarian world. It offers the most ambitious and visible perspectives of intervention, as revealed in a comparison of its active members, superficial as it may be, with those of fragmentary, so-called affinity groups. It exhibits a practical dimension of real intervention not only in the world of labor but also in society, which other organic expressions of libertarian magma lack. It constitutes, furthermore, a bastion against state-sanctioned unionism and its defects, while offering a suggestive project for the future. Émile Pouget stated in 1903, "At present, for the trade unionist the trade union is an organism of conflict and claim of worker against employer. In the future it will be the base on which normal society will be built, when freed from exploitation and oppression."[5]

None of what has been said so far implies that anarcho-syndicalism is without problems. And it is likely that those problems warrant an affirmation so often formulated that suggests that libertarian syndicalism is so much more preferable the less syndicalist it is and the more open to a diversity of tasks. It is not a matter of debating the desirability of unions but rather a matter of breaking through many of the boundaries of the world of labor. And this is so because strictly labor union activity carries with it a range of weaknesses that should not be ignored. Some of these weaknesses were already referred to a hundred years ago by Errico Malatesta. I will cite two of his statements. The first, undoubtedly excessive, emphasizes that "unionism is not, and never will be, anything but a legalistic and conservative

---

5   Waintrop, *Les anarchists espagnols*, 117.

movement, unable to aim beyond—if that far!—the improvement of working conditions."[6] The second argues, "In
the industrial movement the official is a danger comparable
only to parliamentarianism. Any anarchist who has agreed
to become a permanent and salaried official of a trade union
is lost to anarchism."[7]

Beyond Malatesta's views, syndicalism in general—and,
to a lesser degree, anarcho-syndicalism—commonly grants
a radical primacy to the salary and thus forgets—or at least
postpones—important issues. Questions like environmental
and resource limits, the marginalization of women, the submission suffered by the unemployed, or, to be brief, the excesses surrounding consumerism have never, or almost never,
been a priority for labor union activity. The mere fact that
nowadays there are still many unionists who do not understand that a general strike must not only be one of production but also one of consumption clearly expresses my point
on the matter.

There is no shortage of people who, obsessed by salaries
and by the accumulation of goods, consider that the workers'
movement should consider the usefulness of distinguishing
between misery and poverty, prioritizing an emphasis on the
latter over the misery associated with the logic of capitalism,
with the apparently unrestrained goal of increasing wealth
exponentially. From this perspective, we must remember
that in many archaic societies, as well as in many peasant
societies, poverty was, and still often is, a voluntary choice.
François Partant argued, "It concerns the aim of maintaining an equilibrium between the social group and its environment, one of constant limited resources. Or, what's more,
preserving another equilibrium—between the members of
the social group—that avoids an increase of wealth that favors inequalities between them at the expense of the group's

---

6   Errico Malatesta, quoted in Guérin, *Anarchism*, 79.

7   Ibid.

cohesion."[8] From afar, and as is so often the case, it is easy to appreciate the importance of distinguishing between relational benefits—related to our often weak social life—and material benefits.

Self-Management

Although the concept has clearly been around for a long time, the term *self-management* only appeared to gain ground in the 1960s, perhaps as translation, initially into French, of the Serbo-Croatian *samoupravljanje*. Moreover, it is relatively common to suggest that the spreading of the word occurred during the events of May 1968 in France. There is irrefutable proof, however, that the ideas contained in the word *self-management* existed long before its use, evidenced by the resolutions of the CNT congress celebrated in 1919, which speak of the *socialization* of the land and the instruments of production and exchange.[9] Almost twenty years later, the congress that the CNT held in Zaragoza in 1936 defined libertarian communism as a regime, the result of the federation of free and autonomous agrarian and industrial associations, built on the basis of labor unions and free communes.[10] It is also worth remembering that, before the civil war, there existed a remarkable culture of *self-management*—the collectivizations attest to this—that was certainly not exclusive to the libertarian world; many of the organizations affiliated to the Unión General de Trabajadores also participated in it. This culture of self-management has dramatically lost power, as evinced by the fact that two of the current Spanish majority labor unions of Spain, the Comisiones Obreras and the UGT, with hundreds of thousands of members and

---

8   François Partant, quoted in Offensive, *Construire l'autonomie*, 190.

9   See http://www.cntvalladolid.es/IMG/pdf/congresosCNT/IIcongreso
      .pdf.

10   Waintrop, *Les anarchists espagnols*, 296.

significant resources, have been incapable of offering any example of a self-managed organization other than that of a modest travel agency.

At the core of the self-management proposition lies the idea, very dear to our grandparents, that the world can function without bosses but not without workers. Before the primordial aggression that the concentration of private property in the hands of a few presupposes, and before the consequent injustice and inequality, self-management promotes the organization of everyone and not an organization above everyone. And it does so in the most diverse of spheres, particularly in the realm of work, through the parallel defense of federal coordination formulas. In short, it combines the principles of autonomy and equality, embodied in rich and plural communities, and not in monolithic realities. Internal pluralism, diversity of opinions, and their respect are crucial, as is the awareness that nothing good is gained if the resolution of problems is delegated to external authorities.

However, the practice of self-management is not without its difficulties. I will refer to two of them. While the first relates to the people's interest—sometimes, from an objective point of view, they are not interested in participating—the second refers to the real knowledge of things, often quite slight, these same people display. We should ask, though, whether the first of these difficulties has not been intentionally induced by the system and whether the second has not acquired its unusual relevance because we have unjustifiably accepted complex societies that call for experts' help. Whatever the facts, it seems that the fabric of resistance offered by self-management practices is much stronger than those granted by parliamentary parties.

The practice of self-management, thoroughly horizontal and egalitarian, implies for obvious reasons the disappearance of *entrepreneurs*. This is the occasion to note that the corresponding project is unrelated to what has come to be known as "economy of the commons" in recent years, whose essential aim is the attempt to make businessmen assume—always within the rules of reigning capitalism—a measured conduct. The idea of *good entrepreneurship*, however, appears foreign to all libertarian approaches.

V.

SPACES OF AUTONOMY AND THE NEW SOCIETY

Spaces of Autonomy

For a long time, I have defended the idea that building autonomous spaces where we could apply a different set of rules than those imposed on us should be the main task for any movement that sets out to contest capitalism from the double perspective of self-management and decommodification, and certainly away from any intention to compete with the system.

The choice that concerns me is as necessary as it is honorable and feasible. It ultimately rests on the conviction that we must begin to build the society of tomorrow today, with the twofold purpose of urgently exiting capitalism and of outlining structures of grassroots self-management, beyond salaried labor and commodities. For, as Landauer put it so well, in an argument similar to the one mentioned above, "We are the State, and we shall continue to be the State until we have created the institutions that form a real community."[1] I tend to believe that those spaces, which logically must have a capacity to attract and expand, configure a much more realistic project than the one always proposed, more modestly these days, by enlightened social democracy. When someone talks to me about the necessity of creating a public bank, I feel obliged to ask myself how much time we have to wait before this becomes a reality, especially since the proposal in question must necessarily pass, yet again, through the channel of political parties, parliaments, and institutions. Is it more utopian to call for a generalized self-management than to demand a world government or a reform of the International Monetary Fund?

I could add—though it is not really necessary—that these spaces of autonomy of which I speak cannot in any way be isolated examples that embrace a merely individualistic and particularistic project; it is not a matter of creating small states, as Élisée Reclus originally pointed out, or as Jacques Camatte restated a century later. Their perspective ought to be, necessarily and under an expansive affect, that of generalized self-management. And not only that: their introduction cannot leave aside the active and frontal contestation of the system or suppress the struggle against capital and the state. Rather, this project should promote a permanent insurrection in all areas, as many of the propositions coming from radical feminism certainly do. We should not forget also that those who struggle for these spaces have more often than not preserved forms of struggle of older traditions and, far removed from the compromised unionism we see everywhere, currently work in organizations that have always been engaged in this conflict.

It's a simple task to portray, even in summary fashion, some of the objectives autonomous spaces should pursue:

---

1   Gustav Landauer, quoted in Isabelle Fremeaux and John Jordan, *Les sentiers de l'utopie* (Paris: La Découverte, 2012), 364.

putting an end to division of labor, to the *mass worker*, victim of repetitive work, and to the negative consequences of mechanization; recuperating knowledges on the verge of disappearing; restoring an awareness of the meaning of autonomous work, without hierarchies or instructions from above; resuscitating the collective and collaborative element in the face of current atomization; putting an end to the hysteria of competition; finishing with the obsession of unrestrained consumption; distributing work and addressing unemployment; reassessing and distributing domestic work; and lastly, putting an end to *homo economicus* linked to the societies of necessity and not to societies of the gift.[2]

The Debate over Autonomy

The project that I now defend has certainly aroused criticisms that merit both attention and responses. So far it has been said—against all reason, I believe—that it rests on an implicit acceptance of the capitalist order. It is quite surprising that this argument comes from those who have chosen to assume the two alternative paths glimpsed in the world of *left*: the legalist-parliamentarian and the revolutionary-putschist. If in the first case the surprise is obvious, in the second it refers to reasons that should also be evident and that are related to the blatant acceptance of entire imaginary or power: hierarchy, vanguard, and substitution. I don't wish to annoy anyone when I emphasize that these two presumably alternative paths share far too many elements in common. Both lack a reflection on power and alienation. Both elude considering the implications of power in all spheres: family, school, work, science, technology, unions, and political parties. The consequences of complex societies, industrialization, urbanization, and deruralization are ignored in both. The commonly silent acceptance of growth, consumption, and competition

2   Naïma Benabdelali, quoted in Offensive, *Construire l'autonomie*, 160.

is also noticeable in them. And we may also foretell in both the risk of imminent absorption by a system that in fact has never been abandoned. Instead of smiling before what they understand as the utopian naïveté of those who forge autonomous spaces, these individuals would do better to revise their knowledge of history and remember how the first Christians succeeded at the margins of the Roman Empire, how the first incipient capitalist enterprises established themselves in the face of absolutist states, or simply the successes and failures of some socialists, the primitive—wrongly called utopians— and always doomed to oblivion.

I am obliged to add that if this discussion that I bring up today seems very old, its relevance, however, is perhaps far greater than in the past. This is so at least in the eyes of those of us who consider that capitalism has entered a phase of terminal corrosion that, due to climate change, the depletion of primary energy resources, the continuing exploitation of the countries of the global South, the disintegration of precarious safety nets, and the desperate deployment of a new and obscene social Darwinism puts the collapse just around the corner. In the face of this, the response of the two aforementioned alternative paths seems unfortunately weak: if in some cases, little more than the defense of welfare states and a "social exit from the crisis" is called for—or as I have previously suggested, and what amounts to the same, an unreal and sordid return to 2007— in others, this response finds sustenance in the illusion of a self-proclaimed vanguard, invested with the authority granted by a supposed social science, that must decide for all by imitating many of the recorded fiascos of the twentieth century. Failing that, they promote radical anti-capitalist claims that care nothing for documenting how the corresponding project will be carried out. In the end, and in the best of cases, they translate into to an active and respectable day-to-day struggle that, however, has limited consequences.

I know very well that the horizon of autonomy, self-management, and decommodification does not magically resolve all of these problems. It is easy, for example, for many of the schemes of patriarchal society to persist. And one cannot dismiss the possibility that, under those same schemes, competition and the absence of solidarity are reinforced, amid a lingering respect for the rules of capitalism. I can only assert that the horizon that I now defend points us toward a plausible solution. I don't even believe that this horizon lags behind the other options in regard to a thousand-times-repeated discussion, born of the question of whether we are so naive as to conclude that our autonomous spaces will not be the object of the repressive wrath of capital and the state. We are not—we simply limit ourselves to asking our friends who recommend the legal-parliamentarian and revolution-ary-putschist options what defenses they plan for their own projects and whether they are in a position to deploy them, all the more so when, considering the current state of things, it looks less and less likely that they will have something to defend. Are these more solid or credible than ours? Or will it be the case, in the end—and please allow me this malicious-ness—that those who throw themselves into the effort to repress autonomous spaces are those same friends with whom we debate today?

I leave for the end a dispute that is not without interest: whether the project of autonomy and the other two which I have critically glossed are incompatible or whether, on the contrary, they can find some common ground. I will answer in a manner that is both quick and self-interested: if the major consequence of this common ground is that it allows many people to approach liberated spaces, then it is welcome. Yet I fear that we are speaking of diametrically opposing views about what social organization is and what emancipation entails. And I see myself obliged to underscore the enormous flaw in the *traditional left*'s commitments, where there is not even a whiff of self-management and what we do smell, by contrast, is a scenario of hierarchies, representation, and complete reproductions of the world that we supposedly claim to challenge. Although no one has a magic solution to problems, I am more and more convinced that there are some who have chosen to embrace the quickest and most convincing path.

The Future Society

Those versions of anarchism that conceived of revolution as a *moment* in the course of which a well-defined human group—often identified with a social class—would suddenly subvert the existing rules and outline new ones seem to have lost ground. Even though this perspective has acquired, with whatever nuances that we may think of, a kind of legitimacy at certain moments in history, there are more than enough reasons to imagine different horizons, such as those linked to long processes of class struggle accompanied by the progressive gestation of spaces of autonomy, with the presence and participation of less compact human groups than those that seemed to lead many of the rebellions of the past aiming at emancipation. In this respect, and by way of conclusion, there are many who consider that the old distinction between *evolution* and *revolution* has lost its significance. It was Élisée Reclus who argued that revolutionary upheavals are an unequivocal part of a natural evolutionary process. Furthermore, despite some anarchists denying the existence of a transition phase, this is a rather uncommon characteristic of the libertarian project; rather, it is the effort to stress that the characteristics of this phase should adjust themselves thoroughly to the condition of the final objective—something that, we must admit, logically implies a certain weakening of the presumed transition phase. The effort in question is accompanied by the firm conviction that a revolution is the only salvation, not because of a radical drive or a dogmatic stubbornness but rather a simple relational logic.

I have already pointed out that libertarian thought appears mistrustful of the rigor and utility of preestablished theories and deterministic processes. Therefore, it gives no serious credit to the idea that today's reality leads inexorably toward libertarian communism or something similar. It underscores time and again, however, that equality cannot be created by means of instruments—in particular, the state— that by definition embody hierarchy and inequality. It is unthinkable for a free society to arise from decisions taken by a separate bureaucracy, a presumed carrier of special knowledge and virtues. Moreover, the mark of Proudhonian federalism lies at the core of the majority of libertarian projects; that is, the defense of a society articulated federally from below, in which, with the *commune* as its basic unit, decentralization and self-management are procedures that counteract the effects of the concentration of power and the decisions coming from above. Thus, behind all this we may surmise a thorough defense of the full autonomy of individuals and of the institutions they establish, by means of free and voluntary agreements. The book *Anarquismo básico* reminds us that in the second half of the nineteenth century, "anarchists were called not only *antiauthoritarians* and *revolutionary socialists* but also *autonomists* and *federalists*."[3]

In short, the revolution the libertarians have in mind will be, above all, a *social* revolution, and not a *political* one. The Troploin collective states, "Our emancipation will not come except from a revolution that transforms the whole of daily life *at the same time* that it attacks political power and creates its own organs, by means of an insurrection that, combining both a destructive and a creative labor, brings down repressive apparatuses and replaces them with nonmercantile social relations, reaching the point of irreversibility, removing from beings and things their quality of commodities, undermining the bases of bourgeois and state power, and changing structures and materials."[4]

---

3   Fundación Anselmo Lorenzo and Confederación Nacional del Trabajo de Sevilla, *Anarquismo básico* (Madrid: FAL/CNT, 2010), 108.

4   Troploin, *El timón y los remos: Preguntas y respuestas* (Madrid: Editorial

Fotopoulos and Albert

I will now turn my attention to two recent theorizations, authored by Takis Fotopoulos and Michael Albert, that are modestly controversial and that refer to what a libertarian society could be like.[5] It is not a matter of closed conceptions, as one may easily imagine. Do those people demanding exhaustive proposals in economics have, by any chance, anything to offer to us? The market economy, perhaps?

Fotopoulos's perspective is based on advocating a society that is grounded never on imposition but on free and voluntary decisions that allow for the taking of collective decisions, in contrast to the oligarchic politics of today. In this society there would be no institutional structures that could reflect unequal relations of power. Once hierarchical relations are abolished and the primacy of experts shut down, formulas of election by lot will prevail, with full and permanent revocability, in such a way that representation will adjust itself to very strict norms and clearly assigned duties. The assembly will be the principal body of the different communities, coordinated through regional and confederal administrative councils, with delegates nominated with revocable mandates and subject to rotation.

In Fotopoulos's view, democracy will also have to inexorably encompass the economy through communities that are self-sufficient to the greatest possible degree. Property will be collectivized—it will not belong to the workers of any one factory or another—and so will be common resources, assigned in solidarity and in a confederal manner by means of decentralized planning formulas. The *community* will be their deployment unit, and not the productive centers, with a view to satisfying general interests and avoiding criteria favored by

Klinamen, 2012), 82.

5   Takis Fotopoulos, *Towards an Inclusive Democracy* (London: Cassell, 1997); Michael Albert, *Moving Forward: Program for a Participatory Economy* (Oakland: AK Press, 2001).

growth and efficiency. Fotopoulos points out in this regard that cooperatives are not in themselves spaces of full autonomy, to the extent that they can simply be another form of business. Most important are the dimension of integration and the aim of prefiguring the future society on the basis of self-management, mutual aid, and equality.

The model advocated by Fotopoulos would benefit from a notable decentralization, under a wholehearted commitment to smaller political communities, less bureaucratized and closer to the people. Fotopoulos reminds us that the existence of a relation between high levels of income and the reduced size of states can hardly be a mere coincidence. He specifically notes that, at the beginning of the 1990s, 27 of the 45 countries with less than 500,000 inhabitants and 9 of the 13 with less than 100,000 showed high levels of personal income.[6] The functioning of small reclaimed communities will ultimately be characterized by an open, integral pluralism respectful of individual positions. In Fotopoulos's eyes, new technologies can cooperate in the incorporation of formulas of direct democracy and in confederal coordination.

Albert's analysis, for its part, is more detailed than Fotopoulos's regarding the economic dimension of the advocated model. I will content myself here with underlining some of the fundamental principles that sustain it, which in fact are similar to those proposed by Fotopoulos. The work centers, to begin with, should be the property of all citizens, workers and consumers, who would express their preferences through democratic councils present at all levels in a scenario of participatory planning. Elsewhere, the current division of labor, coupled with rooted hierarchies and repetitive tasks, should be rejected. Remuneration shall reflect the effort employed, the time invested, and the sacrifices assumed. The participatory economy postulated by Albert "represents a structure fleshed out through councils and information

---

6   Fotopoulos, *Towards an Inclusive Democracy*, 244.

exchange so as to arrive at flexible libertarian planning arrangements which are continually open to the changing conditions and the preferences of consumers and workers."[7] This proposal, of a visibly pragmatic character, aims primarily at liberation in the economy; that is, the postulation of a society free of the economy, just as Malatesta certainly envisioned it.

---

7   Luciano Lanza, quoted in Graham, *A Documentary History of Libertarian Ideas, Volume 3*, 308–9.

VI.

HISTORY AND CONFRONTATIONS

Our Libertarians

During the celebrations for the centenary of the CNT's foundation in 2010 it was not infrequent to witness among media circles of power many attempts at demystification of what was for us the libertarian movement. Although demystification is always healthy, to do it with something that was formerly and systematically forgotten is striking, much more so when those responsible for it display little interest in freeing themselves from the demonizing clichés that they themselves forged or, in this case, inherited. In the heat of this bewildering ceremony, some of the habits embraced by the republican bourgeoisie three quarters of a century ago have reappeared in the form of a contemptuous intellectualism and a commiserating paternalism that are applied to those who, then as now, are *the invisible*.

Our libertarians had their share of flaws, of course. If among them a vanguard often functioned in separation from an apathetic base, the absence of serious plans about the future and the contradictions of participation in the political game were frequently accompanied by a sterile revolutionary gymnastics and, with it, a gratuitous violence. None of this, however, justifies setting aside the enormous merits of a movement that dignified the working class, put into place a model egalitarianism in favor of the most disadvantaged, grew without officials or bureaucracies, contributed efficient instruments of resistance and pressure, developed active networks in the form of farms, workshops, and cooperatives, put into place bold educational and cultural initiatives, and ultimately revealed, in extremely difficult circumstances, a formidable capacity for mobilization. The CNT, in addition, played an essential role in curbing the armed [fascist] uprising of July 1936, had a prominent place, over the months that followed, in the experiences of collectivization (something that would be good for our youth to learn about), and suffered a savage repression at the hands of the new regime. Several highly recommendable studies capture this world of social turmoil and permanent struggle: *La cultura anarquista a Catalunya*, by Ferran Aisa; *We, the Anarchists!*, by Stuart Christie; *Venjança de classe*, by Xavier Diez; *Anarchism and the City*, by Chris Ealham; *Anarquistas* by Dolors Marin; and *La revolución libertaria*, by Heleno Saña.[1]

---

1 Ferran Aisa, *La cultura anarquista a Catalunya* (Barcelona: Ediciones 1984, 2006); Stuart Christie, *¡Nosotros, los anarquistas! Un estudio de la Federación Anarquista Ibérica (FAI) 1927–1937*, translated by Sofía Moltó Llorca (Valencia: Universitat de València, 2010) originally published as *We, the Anarchists! A Study of the Iberian Anarchist Federation (FAI) 1927–1937* (Oakland: AK Press, 2008); Xavier Diez, *Venjança de classe* (Barcelona: Virus, 2010); Chris Ealham, *La lucha por Barcelona* (Madrid: Alianza, 2005); Dolors Marin, *Anarquistas* (Barcelona: Ariel, 2010); Heleno Saña, *La revolución libertaria* (Pamplona: Laetoli, 2010). Ealham's book is the Castilian version of the English text *Anarchism and the City: Revolution and Counter-Revolution in Barcelona, 1898–1937*,

I shall, nonetheless, return to the official discourse, always associated with a shameful exercise in presentism: what happened in the past is judged on the basis of the values that—supposedly—are ours today. Nothing then is simpler than to forget the extreme conditions of work and repression that made themselves felt in the 1930s, just as there is nothing simpler than to equate the violence of the system with that of those who suffered it. There is nothing more reasonable than to take as proven the reformist character of the Second—workers'?—Republic—while also forgetting the repression that ensued—not only during the *black biennium* or *bienio negro*—the systematic breach of approved laws, and the frequent silent acceptance of many of the rules of the past. Therefore, from the comfort of the present, there is nothing more logical than to set good unionists against bad anarchists, while at the same time presenting overwhelming evidence of the fortunate participation of the CNT in the traditional political game, stigmatizing everything that smells of social revolution as anachronistic and contemptible, and turning libertarians into those bearing the greatest responsibility for the troubles of the Republic.

A vivid example is expressed in the worn-out contrast between violent anarchists—often presented as genuine delinquents, responsible for so many deaths—and neat militants of left-wing parties, who always maintained their composure. Santos Juliá wrote in the pages of *El País* at the time that "the slaughters in the ranks of the *franquistas* during the civil war were not carried out by republicans, but rather by supporters of a social revolution that, had it triumphed, would also have implied the end of the Republic."[2] Josep Fontana, in his pseudo reply in *Público*,[3] notably opted to avoid the main debate: interested in separating the violence of the franquistas

which I cite profusely further on.

2 *El País*, June 25, 2010.

3 *Público*, June 29, 2010.

and that of the republicans, he chose to answer with silence regarding what can only be understood as Juliá's acritical and classist demonization of the social revolution, accompanied by a canonization of the Republic, as apparent source of all that is good. This type of discourse is, furthermore, very frequent in the collective book authored by a handful of historians, more or less associated with the *official left*, and published in the beginning of 2012 to oppose the manipulations of the Royal Academy of History.[4]

As regards presentism, it always rests on a complete acceptance of the presumed goodness of the order we enjoy today. From this perspective, it is possible to comprehend that another prestigious historian, José Álvarez Junco, who apparently has never heard of the Scala Affair—the Barcelona fire of 1978 in which an attempt was made to lay the blame on the libertarian movement—allows himself to assert that the CNT did not recover after 1975 due to its incapacity to accept the sacred rules of the transition. If everyone is free to express their opinions, it would be better to keep a distance from those who offer such opinions as the distinguished product of a sharp and scientific work, behind which endless prejudices, as well as biased and ideological versions of history, are concealed.

The last of the stigmas of this pathetic discourse is the repeated assertion that anarchism ceased to exist in 1939. To give the lie to it, it is necessary to consider a vast array of information. Let us remember that anarcho-syndicalism is still alive and present, however much the disinformation media prefer to continue to associate it with picket lines and violence. The mark of libertarian thought is also easily discernible in new social movements—feminism, environmentalism, pacifism—and the very new—the worlds of anti-globalization, degrowth, or *indignation*. Many of these

---

4   Ángel Viñas, ed., *En el combate por la historia* (Madrid: Pasado y Presente, 2012).

movements' strategies, which may appear to us to be extremely innovative, were developed—as I will immediately attempt to show—in the libertarian world eighty years ago. The urgency, on the other hand, of responding to the endless collapse of social democracy and Leninism has brought back to discussion words such as *self-management, socialization,* and *decentralization* in support of societies that are not based on coercion or the search for profit and that are suspicious of the supposedly liberating potential of technology. Against these facts, the assertion that anarchism is an ideology of the past, so common in palace sermons, reveals rather well the time in which those who express it live.

The Republican Myth

The only serious reason that invites us to lend any support to the republican option is the corruption of the monarchy we live under. This option, however, often presupposes that the most important problems that burden us are closely and exclusively tied to the monarchical institution. As if a republic would magically solve them all! Nevertheless, it is necessary to bear in mind that the majority of the member states of the European Union are republics, without this being in itself a guarantee of anything relevant.

It is certainly true that, in the Spanish case, the demand for a republic not only sinks its roots in an awareness of the conditions of the actually existing monarchy, it is also based on the desire to return dignity to the political regime that reigned in the 1930s. Even though such a desire is highly respectable—how can the teachers of the Republic not be honored, and how can one not remember those who fought fascism?—it would be good if people who wish to give it free reign also kept their distance from something that ultimately seems, even in this case, like a delicate process of inventing a tradition.

And we do the truth no favors if we avoid criticisms of the Second Republic. I am clearly not referring here to those poured by the *revisionist* literature of the ultramontanist right: I am thinking of those criticisms that touch the raw nerve of how the Republic served to ground the interests of an ascendant bourgeoisie that did not hesitate to point its sharp instruments of repression against those popular classes it supposedly wished to educate. I think also of how it left things as they were in decisive respects in the end, or in the necessity to disable myths that have been forged with time around such equivocal personalities as Azaña and Ortega—the first being portrayed as a statesman, bearer of a modernizing national project and in no way associated with the ascendant bourgeoisie mentioned above, while the second is described bluntly as an impeccable democrat, Europeanist, federalist, and tolerant.

It will be wise not to lose sight of the fact that we often place many people under the general category of *republicans*, who, from the perspective of a final social revolution, struggled in favor of other horizons. "The republican police is like the monarchist police, just as republican tyranny is the same as that of the monarchy. The police is unchanged, nor will it change. Its mission was, is and will continue to be the persecution of workers and the poor," an editorial in *Solidaridad Obrera* stated with sharp clarity in 1932.[5]

The Years of War

Allow me to dedicate some time to give my opinion on what libertarians did in the years of the Spanish Civil War, a moment in which the workers, or many of them, confronted fascism head-on; something that their German, Italian, or French counterparts did not do—or did only with far less daring.

---

5   *Solidaridad Obrera*, September 9, 1932, cited in Chris Ealham, *Anarchism and the City: Revolution and Counter-Revolution in Barcelona, 1898–1937* (Oakland: AK Press, 2010), 124.

It is well known that in those years an acute and intense polemic took place between those who argued that the war and the revolution had to be carried out simultaneously—in substance, the libertarians—and those who asserted that the only priority was being victorious in the war. The scenario was particularly hostile for the former, who certainly suffered the effects of the war but also the harassment, the boycott, and the lack of collaboration, in many cases, of the republican authorities and the political forces that backed them. The party of order, as its name states, assumed an unabashed defense of the established order, symbolically expressed in the devolution to their owners of many of the industries and lands that had been collectivized at the beginning of the war. As a result, in the decades that followed, the experiment of collectivization, carried out voluntarily in the majority of cases by industrial workers and peasants without hierarchical structures, fell into oblivion, along with the republicans' endeavors against it.

Little attention has been given to the fact that many of the Russian debates from two decades earlier reemerged in Spain in 1936. Were the conditions ripe for a revolution in the country? A good part of the Leninist historiography that had answered affirmatively to this question in regard to Russia seemed to understand that in Spain, by contrast, the conditions were absent, to such an extent that the sign of apparent revolution registered in 1936 would have rather been the product of the failure, albeit relative, of the military uprising than the consequence of an objectively suitable scenario for revolution. It was easy to suspect a hidden prosaic fact: the prospect of a revolution in Spain was scorned because it would barely be controlled and directed by those who were putting forth the argument against it. The libertarian response, of course, revealed itself to be far less imbued with objective certainties and far more inclined to identifying various possibilities derived from complex circumstances (and not only from the military coup).

As things were, some of the versions of Leninist critique—
and by this I am not referring to the Spanish Communist
Party's *official* discourse—were in agreement in pointing out
that the anarchists should have taken power in 1936 (we
could conclude that the Leninists believed, in their own way,
in the Spanish libertarian movement, for which they seemed
to display a subterranean admiration; otherwise, they would
never have suggested that a rival assumed governments and
ministries). Certainly, anarchists never unilaterally and exclusively took power—in this they were consistent—just as
it is certain that on the ground, and at least in its directive
helm—for an entity of this nature did finally develop—they
abandoned the full deployment of a grassroots revolution
and often entered into open contradiction with the very
principles they declared as their own. This curious way of
proceeding resulted in a very peculiar scenario: while, on
the one hand, it was emphasized that the libertarians were
people whom it was not convenient to trust—an obstacle in
the path of republican order—on the other, it was usually
forgotten that the CNT essentially did what it was asked. It
incorporated itself, in particular, to the Catalan and Spanish
governments, with well-known results: an accumulation of
difficulties for internal democracy, where an incipient bureaucracy settled and in which debate was nonexistent. Not
only did it fail to gain any benefit for its cause, it would also
soon come to admit the magnitude of the error committed.
It acted with a naive generosity that others did nothing to
reciprocate: let us not forget that, during the civil war, the
conduct of the libertarian world was infinitely less aggressive
and planned than the power apparatus of the Republic and
its supporters. Against this backdrop, and as far as I can see,
the record of those years—when an extraordinary combination of the most beautiful experiment and the most colossal
error took place—did not demonstrate the ineptitude of the
anarchist project but rather the terrible consequences of its
abandonment.

Why should we accept—and here I return to the theoretical discussion of the grounds for a potential Spanish revolution—the supposed error of singularity, of the anomaly, of an anarchism and an anarcho-syndicalism that thrived after the First World War? Did others fare much better? Was not this anomaly a principal explanation for why it took three years for fascism to sink its roots in the greater part of the Iberian Peninsula? Are we not, in the end, under the obligation to do away with many of the stigmas that have been fixed on Spanish libertarians? In this respect, I am glad to see that some professional historians have begun to acknowledge this, even though our anarchists never developed a millenarian movement—not even in the south of the peninsula—and even though there is no reason to disqualify a priori such a commitment. It would seem the promising beginning of revisionism.

The CNT Example

Chris Ealham's book, already referred to above, offers precious information with respect to the kind of action developed by the CNT over a quarter century in a singular location: the city of Barcelona. It portrays, first and foremost, a revolutionary transformation of space and control of public life,[6] with a sharp consciousness of community and local autonomy,[7] a noteworthy effort directed toward rendering neighborhoods impenetrable, independent, and mutually supporting,[8] and finally, the deployment of practices of a profoundly democratic nature. What was revealed behind all this was the aim of enforcing a morality superior to that of the bourgeois, commonly perceived as criminals, and under the aegis of a very active movement of denunciation of

---

6 Ealham, *Anarchism and the City*, 36.

7 Ibid., 41.

8 Ibid.

what alcohol, prostitution, religious institutions, bullfights, or sexual repression entailed. The most significant result was a collective and elated *we* confronting property-owning classes who impeded the satisfaction of vital necessities,[9] such as those related to clothing, food, and shelter.[10] A *we* that is also coupled with an explicit defense of illegality, understood as "anarchist and revolutionary."[11] "I am a pure anarchist and I rob banks, yet I am incapable of robbing the poor, like others do," stated one of the thieves of an armory.[12]

Libertarian Barcelona would often flaunt its support for self-management practices. Let us remember, for example, that in the 1919 CNT congress it was proposed that vacant lands be expropriated and new buildings be constructed by union labor. Although in a different domain, Termes reminds us that graphic arts labor unions were incited to apply a *red censorship* over those publications that misinformed on matters related to questions of labor.[13] Is this even imaginable among the majority labor unions in Spain today? Furthermore, many initiatives that appear to us strictly contemporary were tried by our anarchist and anarcho-syndicalist grandparents, very knowledgeable in the meaning of direct action. I speak of strikers and the unemployed who would refuse to pay in restaurants; of protected groups of women who would rob shops; or of more delicate operations, like robberies of banks or to those transporting money and payrolls. There were also frequent protests organized to reduce the cost of housing and food. Let us not forget that there also existed a Tenants Union (Sindicato de Inquilinos), which in 1922 managed to call a strike in collaboration with the construction workers. House occupations were the order of the day, as well as

---

9   Ibid., 39.

10 Ibid., 159.

11 Ibid., 126.

12 Ibid., 117.

13 Termes, *Història del movement anarquista a Espanya*, 306.

what we would call today *escraches* in front of the homes of large property owners.[14] That the initiatives went beyond the realm of work is laid bare by the fact that in the 1930s the Economic Defense Commission (Comisión de Defensa Económica) proposed increasing efforts to make workers aware of consumption problems in the face of speculative, rentier, and commercial interests, coupled with numerous complaints about the low quality of the goods produced or demands related to schools, health centers, public lighting, and transportation.

Another of the characteristics of libertarian practice was its clearly inclusive nature. In situations where respect for older generations was proverbial, a constant preoccupation with the problems of the unemployed was also evident. Groups of unemployed who sought work were frequently put together, and thus they collectively exercised a certain pressure on business owners. The CNT also organized its own employment offices that aimed at pressing bosses and controlling their practices, and it was often the means of entry and integration into the cities for arriving immigrants. Libertarians were also prone to rejecting those categories whose purpose in prison was to distinguish between political, social, and common prisoners. It seems hard to assert, however, that things developed along the same lines with respect to women, who were regular victims of marginalization and were commonly relegated to secondary roles.

The libertarian world, I shall add, also generated a rich network of support in the area of culture and propaganda. By this I am referring to associations, athenaeums—with spaces that offered products at reduced prices or that scheduled musical and theatrical events, further examples of what I have called *spaces of autonomy* elsewhere in this book: rationalist schools—dedicated to literacy and cultural dissemination, cooperatives, workshops, farms, newspapers, publishing

---

14 *Escraches* are public denunciations [editor].

houses, libraries, and excursion and naturalist clubs. What still remains to be studied is the very solid relation with the world of culture, written culture in particular, which has always been displayed by so many libertarians, who undoubtedly managed to rise above the horizon that a society burdened by injustice and inequality had prepared for them. Ealham states that, under the umbrella of the CNT, this dense fabric allowed the forging of an autonomous proletarian culture capable of resisting the influx exercised in so many other places by instruments of mass culture that, in the realm of sports and music, eroded the vigor of socialist consciousness.[15]

Marx and His Followers

I find little pleasure in the obscenely identitarian arguments that have so often marked the relation—or, better put, the rivalry—between libertarians and Marxists. If I have always felt disturbed by the petulance of many of the latter, supposed bearers of a terribly complex social science that calls for high priests, I also find no comfort before certain discourses that, from a libertarian point of view, escape any critical discussion of important matters.

Therefore, we first need to distinguish between the different kinds of Marxists. It is quite clear that there is little relation between, on the one hand, an arrogant Leninist who believes, with a military spirit, in the redeeming Party and recklessly wields the same old phraseology and, on the other, the heterodox Marxists who in many cases have been influenced by—and have duly acknowledged this—a libertarian stream. Although choosing specific examples provokes in me a certain discomfort, I can refer to those that, seemingly open-minded and open to dialogue, often flaunt dramatic silences. A superficial example: the book *The Idea of Communism*, by Tariq

---

15 Ealham, *Anarchism and the City*, 47.

Ali.[16] The text does not do justice to its title, however, given that it barely pays attention to *the idea* of communism. Ali's work simply identifies the latter with Marx and Engels's thought and the thought of those who have claimed allegiance to them, ignoring any consideration of the communist currents that flowed through other channels, in particular the libertarian (it is pointless for the reader to search in those pages, for instance, for any mention of Bakunin, Kropotkin, or Malatesta). Ali sidesteps all discussion of the state, does the impossible to save Lenin's and Trotsky's faces—all evils find their source in Stalinism—ignores the criticisms that the Soviet and Chinese experiments received from anarchist premises or from heterodox Marxism itself, and ultimately, and probably without wanting to, feeds the idea that to gauge what communism is, it is sufficient to resolve the question of what the Soviet-type systems actually were.

I willingly accept, nonetheless, that to determine what Marx said and did is not always a simple task. If I were to begin with the good side of the German thinker, I would point out that the anti-statist dimension of Marx and Engels's thought has been ignored a thousand times over. I will refer in this case to the Engels who wrote *The Origin of the Family, Private Property and the State* and who rightly stated, "The society which organizes production anew on the basis of a free and equal association of the producers will put the whole state machinery where it will then belong—into the museum of antiquities, next to the spinning wheel and the bronze ax."[17] And I will emphasize that the explanation of the concept—quite infrequent in Marx's work—of *dictatorship of the proletariat* has been abused. Thus, I shall ask: where are those Marxists who forget that Marx often defined socialism as a

16 Tariq Ali, *La idea del comunismo* (Madrid: Alianza, 2012).

17 Friederich Engels, quoted in Wayne Price, *The Abolition of the State: Anarchist & Marxist Perspectives* (Bloomington, IN: AuthorHouse, 2007), 3.

federation of free communes and not as a bureaucratized and centralized state, which, as far as I am concerned, drastically separates his views from those brandished by Lenin beginning in 1917? I will confess, however, that to present Marx as a libertarian thinker is to do violence to reality, regardless of how much the *Economic and Philosophic Manuscripts of 1844*—with the theory of alienation—and *The Civil War in France* are profusely cited (just as Lenin's *The State and Revolution* is also cited). The careful anthology of Marx's and Engels's *libertarian* thought by Carlos Díaz published a few years ago seems to confirm this to me, albeit not without a paradox.[18]

Yet this may also be perhaps a good occasion to remember that the anarchist contemporaries of Marx—most significantly, Bakunin—seemed to have accepted the essence of his critique of political economy, often emphasizing that such an acceptance was largely due to the idea that this critique was rooted in concepts already grounded in the practice of the workers' movement of the time.[19] What has often been described as a gesture of intellectual openness by Bakunin—the celebrated acceptance of Marxist political economy—may also be interpreted as an unforgiveable carelessness. Nevertheless, the principal theorists of nineteenth-century anarchism failed to develop a critique of political economy that could respond in a more refined way to the conceptual presuppositions of anarchism, an option that today seems quite delicate to us, even if we acknowledge that none of these nineteenth-century anarchist theorists sought to deploy a macro worldview as Marx aspired to do.

Even though a large part of Marx's theorizations about wage labor, commodities, or surplus value merit everyone's attention, there are, as far as I can see, five significant lacunae in Marx's proposition: an ignorance with regard to many of the oppressions and alienations that we suffer and, hence,

18 Carlos Díaz (ed.), *Marx-Engels: El libro rojo y negro* (Gijón: Júcar, 1976).
19 Graeber, *Direct Action*, 211, fn. 5.

what this implies about the roots of emancipation; a dramatic idealization of the development of the productive forces as sources of prosperity and justice; the intuition that the material resources available to us are inexhaustible; the incapacity to take cognizance of the exploitation and marginalization specific to women; and, lastly, an unrestrained Jacobinism. In the back room, and in a plan burdened by the defense of aberrant formulas of centralization that—and I will say it again— owe so much to the presumption of possessing a social science that should be managed by a group of specialists, a kind of Marxism has surreptitiously exalted—stolen, actually—the word *socialism* as if it were the supreme expression of its wager, in the same way that capitalism has enjoyed identifying itself, with vested interest, with democracy.

Power: The Soviet Experiment

If there is any meaning in discussing Marx's affinities and choices, the presumed realization of his thought in what became known as "Soviet-type systems" leaves little room to maneuver.

The first thing worth reviewing here is the perspicacious lucidity of many anarchist analyses that cautioned against the possible consequences of applying Marx's ideas. I speak of possible deviations because, indeed, the relation between the Marx's work and what Lenin did with it is controversial, to such an extent that there is no good reason to attribute to the former many of the decisions assumed by the latter. In a similar way, it would be naive to confuse Lenin with Stalin, as well as to conclude that the first had nothing to do with the scenario outlined by his successor in regard to the management of the Soviet state. With respect to the latter, I certainly do not include myself among those who reckon that the majority of the miseries that this state has caused were the product of Stalinism's maliciousness: the seed had been planted by Lenin with the cancelation of the soviets' independent power, the decision to proscribe other political alternatives, the aberrant centralizing project that served as foundation for a nascent bureaucracy, the rehabilitation of a good part of the imperial logic of czarism, or, in sum, a sui generis interpretation of what Marx had understood regarding what should be the development of capitalism and social formations.

I come back nevertheless to the anarchist analyses by appealing to three examples. The first is from Bakunin: "The leaders of the Communist party, namely Mr. Marx and his followers, will proceed to liberate humanity in their own way. They will concentrate the reins of government in a strong hand…. They will establish a single state bank, concentrating in its hands all commercial, industrial, agricultural, and even scientific production, and then divide the masses into two armies—industrial and agricultural—under the direct command of state engineers, who will constitute a new privileged scientific and political class."[20] The second is from Tolstoy, despite him being a kind of reluctant anarchist: "Even if that should happen which Marx predicted, then the only thing that will happen is that despotism will be passed on. Now the capitalists are ruling, but then the directors of the working class will rule."[21] And the third is from Diego Abad de Santillán, who in this case wrote a posteriori, "Either the revolution gives social wealth to the producers, or it does not. If it does, the producers organize themselves for collective production and distribution and there is nothing left for the State to do. If it does not give social wealth to the producers, the revolution is nothing but a deception and the State goes on."[22]

It is not difficult to summarize in a few words what I believe the Soviet-type systems wound up becoming: a form of bureaucratic state capitalism, dramatically incapable of

---

20 Mikhail Bakunin, quoted in Avrich, *Anarchist Portraits*, 12.

21 Leo Tolstoy, quoted in Marshall, *Demanding the Impossible*, 379.

22 Diego Abad de Santillán, quoted in Guérin, *Anarchism*, 26.

transcending the historical and social universe of canonical capitalism. And under it a new tyranny developed, wage labor and commodities failed to disappear, the power of grassroots revolutionary organizations—the soviets—was annihilated, and, with it, any perspective of self-management was evaporated, a bureaucracy emerged that transformed itself into a kind of collective capitalist, and, as a result, no social revolution took form. Moreover, a working class that would have been head of the new state was invented and idealized—how much more interesting it is to study the deviations of the soviets than it is to analyze the palace intrigues of the Bolsheviks—a clear idealization of the virtues attributed to the development of productive forces gained ground, and, in a scenario in which all dissidence was annihilated—*national* dissidence included—the repression and military power reached enormous levels, and a formidable idolatry of the state took shape, clearly oblivious to many of Marx's theorizations in this regard. If someone wishes to add that external pressure had a significant influence on the establishment of all these elements, I would happily agree, understanding, however, that this can hardly justify the results: it would be unwarranted to categorically state that an intentionally revolutionary process must always end up transformed into something else—either through loss of momentum or through authoritarian radicalization and state idolatry—as a consequence of the pressure exerted by the order against which it is mobilized.

Many of the excesses of the Soviet-type systems found their realization in an institution: the leading single party, where the utmost degree of a hierarchical perspective found its expression. Holloway describes it as a sort of disciplining of the class struggle, by virtue of which the latter's endless expressions are subordinated to state control.[23] Such an impoverishment of class struggle was not limited to the different forms of expression of Leninist, Trotskyist, or Stalinist

---

23 Holloway, *Change the World without Taking Power*, 17.

discourse; on the contrary, it extends to all of those projects whose aim is the conquest of political power—that is, to all of those projects incapable of forging themselves without hierarchies and leaders.

The Collapse of Social Democracy

At this stage, it no longer seems to make any real sense to critically evaluate social democracy: it has itself contributed to its own discredit in powerful ways. If a hundred years ago there still remained a small glimmer for thinking that the ideology promoted by Bernstein or Kautsky aimed at overcoming capitalism, the illusions in this respect have waned over the course of the twentieth century. In the best of cases—and I emphasize "in the best of cases," because circumstances have very often been evidently worse—the objective of social democracy, a project in fact circumscribed to Western Europe, was to manage capitalism in a civilized manner. Even though nowadays there are still many who long for the era of welfare states, I very much fear that the balance of the golden age of social democracy is something less flattering: the obstacles it placed in the path of predatory capitalism were minor; it fed a handful of myths that today cannot but be felt empty—civil society, citizenism, representative democracy; it did not hesitate to comply with all the misery associated with concepts such as growth and competitiveness; it promoted a delicate social demobilization; it linked its name to a particular entity, the famous welfare states, which I have already attempted to explain above; and, finally, it propitiated the development of new forms of colonial domination. All this was forged—let us not forget—in the era of the fat cows, in the years of cheap oil, at the hands of a mental narrative that, under a formidable effort of propaganda and at this scale of self-adulation, we must admit, somehow managed to work.

Subsequent events came to show that there is not much difference, despite the appearances, between the civilized management of capitalism and being carried away by its avalanche in its most savage and unregulated form. In the last quarter-century, social democracy has diluted itself in the magma of the liberal order, even in that of neoliberalism, and it has thereby lost its already precarious markers of identity. The corresponding political project, if it can be called that, is an indelible and singularly pathetic part of this order, to such an extent that it in no way proposes overcoming it. The consequence is easy to discern: the main debate—an easy one to win—with those who still continue to uphold a social democratic horizon, is the one concerning the whereabouts of the political forces capable of expressing its demands. Behind this dispute, of course, is another: one that is born out of the understanding that the survivors of the shipwreck of social democracy, permeated to unimaginable extremes by the logic of the system we live under, soaked in private property and the market, hardly seem able to address the essential problem of the planet's environmental and resource limitations. It is as if they lived in 1930s Washington or 1963 Stockholm and had not taken notice of the fact that the very heart of Keynesian politics, equally idolatrous of the state, has been indelibly damaged by this problem.

Things being what they are, an evident conclusion arises: the deviation of Leninism and of social democracy has become a central element in the inspiration of anarchist ideas. The least that can be said is that in a scenario marked by the ruin of Soviet-type systems—I know already that such a ruin is nothing more than that of Leninism—and the collapse of social democracy, anarchist ideas have ended up visibly less affected and in much better shape. Although there is no reason to exclude the possible reemergence of projects that appeal, to a greater or lesser degree, to social democracy or Leninism, an accumulation of information has been feeding the certainty about how these reborn projects will turn out: far from any emancipatory perspective or any serious awareness of what the collapse entails. This is what one should expect from political forces that, while employing an apparently radical verbal arsenal—perhaps a legacy of their former Leninist affinities—do not hesitate in maintaining alliances with a fully compromised social democracy and its labor union wings, abiding fully with the institutional game, rejecting any project that sustains even a distant relation with self-management, and, imbued with an aberrant short-termism, preferring to close their eyes to the evidence that, as I have just noted, the social democratic vulgate provides no answer to the coming collapse.

The Latin American Models

The exhaustion of social democracy and Leninism has brought with it—perhaps inevitably—the emergence of projects that seek to be different from those born of these two worldviews. The debate is an open one: do the leftist governments of Latin America offer an inspirational model that could provide answers to the many dead ends that we find ourselves facing here in the opulent global North, or, on the contrary, despite the fanfare, should we remain cautious about what these governments represent? Let us not forget that, for many who support the first idea, experiments like those of Venezuela, Ecuador, or Bolivia demonstrate the possibility of respecting the norms of liberal democracy—there are reasonably pluralistic elections in these countries—while simultaneously implementing social policies that are changing the situation, truly and fortunately, in favor of the disadvantaged. Certainly, much of the support that these models incite would respond to at least two distinct perceptions: while for some their greatest virtue would derive from the absence of the vices of *real socialism*, for others, closer to the organic and dogmatic ideas of *Third International communism*, it would rather be the fortunate continuity of what Soviet-type models have, at all levels, always implied.

Before taking up this subject, allow me to say that, from my perspective, this is not a matter of denying that these governments have outlined policies preferable to those of their predecessors. It would be equally problematic to dogmatically and aprioristically reject all they signify, especially given the relief they provide from harassment suffered at the hands of the powerful. Lastly, it would be unwise to close our eyes to certain possibly stimulating tendencies that appeal to options of self-management or to projects linked not to governments but rather to indigenous communities and their unique forms of organization and conduct.

Having said that, however, and to get directly to the most important point, I believe we are obliged to ask ourselves whether experiences like those of Venezuela, Ecuador, or Bolivia constitute suggestive and convincing examples for those of us who find inspiration in a libertarian worldview. And the answer, which to me seems obvious, is negative. And this is so, as it were, for five reasons.

The first of these reasons regards the visibly personalist character of the models here under discussion, built primarily from top to bottom and, in some cases, also dependent on the armed forces. In the libertarian world, where a proud and explicit rejection of leaderships and personalisms exists, projects that evidently move in an opposing direction hardly find any acceptance.

Second, I shall underline that this is not just a matter of leaderships and hierarchies: the other side of the issue has to do with the weakness of the formulas that, in the Latin American models, should permit not only grassroots control but also the full development of projects of self-management. To this may be added the many illusions that derive from the open acceptance of the rules of the game, which refer to liberal democracy, particularly from one of these rules: that which holds that there is nothing wrong with delegating our decision-making ability to others.

Third, the state is almost everything in these models. It is expected that an institution inherited from the old powers should operate in the service of projects whose emancipatory potential, I am afraid, is significantly weighed down. Under this new optical illusion, it is hardly surprising, then, that the typical vices of bureaucratization and corruption still survive.

Fourth, I am obliged to draw attention to the existence of an obvious confusion regarding the underlying condition of the majority of the projects embraced by the leftist governments of Latin America. These projects have almost always pointed in the direction of an amplification of the welfare functions of the institution of the state. Nothing would be more unfortunate than to confuse this with socialism (unless, of course, we remove from this notion much of the richness associated with its meaning). If, on the one hand, there is no record of any socialization of property—or, in the best of cases, such socialization has been marginal—on the other hand, despite the myriad obstacles they have been subjected to, the rules of the market and of capitalism have unequivocally survived.

I will allow myself a fifth and final observation: even in the cases where the participation of indigenous communities in certain institutional projects may have somewhat reduced this concern, the experiences I have been describing have commonly and sadly succumbed to the spell of productivist and developmentalist projects that seem to mimetically reproduce many of the miseries that the opulent global North has exported, more often than not, with reasonable success.

Let us return to the main argument: even if there is no great doubt that leftist Latin American governments have contributed—some more, some less—to the improvement of the conditions of the popular classes, it would seem necessary, from a libertarian perspective, to remain cautious. And this for one principal reason: the certainty that, with the tools these governments have deployed, it is extremely difficult to imagine the establishment of future societies characterized by equality, self-management, decommodification, and respect for the rights of the generations to come. Yet nothing would please me more than to be mistaken.

VII.

NEW AIRS

Cross-Fertilizations

It is very common to consider, with many ambiguities, that the three major manifestations of what became known as *new social movements* are feminism, environmentalism, and what was has sometimes been described as pacifism or, other times, antimilitarism. Years ago, when I set out on the task of giving shape to an anthology of libertarian thought, I must confess I encountered some serious problems when it came to tracing the presence of the material and conceptual foundations of feminism and environmentalism—not so, however, for pacifism/antimilitarism—among the classics of nineteenth-century anarchism, to the extent that I feel tempted to improvise a quick conclusion: the frequent and lucid reflections about the condition of women and our precarious place in

the natural world have rather come—late, for that matter—
from individuals who should be labeled as *libertarians* rather
than *anarchists*, in the strict sense of the word, following the
categorization I proposed earlier and to which I appeal to
throughout this book.

All in all, it is important to understand what I wish to say:
even though the presence of feminism and environmentalism
has been weak in anarchist thought for a very long time—
just as it has been, in a similar fashion, with Marx and his
epigones—it does not mean that it did not carry through the
pertinent revisions with reasonable success, as I will attempt
to document. And it also does not mean that there are serious
obstacles for mutual inspiration today.

Anarchism and Feminism

Despite what I have just said, there exist relatively important
considerations about women and their problems among anarchist thinkers and movements of the past, even if they are
often sporadic and not always fully lucid.

I will begin by recalling that Bakunin rejected patriarchy
on many occasions and denounced "the despotism of the
husband, the father, and the eldest brother over the family,"
something that turned it "into a school of violence and tri-
umphant bestiality, of cowardice and the daily perversions of
the family home."[1] "My father had been quite rich. He was,
in the language of the time, owner of a thousand male souls,
for women were not counted in slavery, in the same way that
they also do not count in freedom today," added Bakunin.[2]

---

1   Mikhail Bakunin, quoted in Graham, *A Documentary History of
     Libertarian Ideas, Volume 3*, 494.

2   Arthur Lehning, *Conversaciones con Bakunin*, trans. Enrique Hegewicz
     (Barcelona: Anagrama, 1978), 16. Originally published as *Michel
     Bakounine et les autres: esquisses et portraits contemporains d'un révolu-
     tionnaire* (Paris: Union Générale d'Éditions, 1976).

In 1872, a Spanish anarchist congress proclaimed, moreover, the equality of women and men, both at home and in work places, a principle very often expressed by Bakunin himself, which in theory at least was later endorsed by anarcho-syndicalism. There was certainly no shortage of competing opinions, such as those voiced, in the wake of Proudhon, by Ricardo Mella. While very suggestive in so many other fields, he believed women should essentially give themselves over to reproduction and care of the home. I would like to add that even though it was common for Spanish anarcho-syndicalists to assume that the abolition of private property would by itself lead to the emancipation of women, there were positions—minority positions, however—that advocated the creation of specific organizations dedicated to struggling for this emancipation, distrustful of the identification invoked above.[3]

Nevertheless, it seems reasonable to stress that the questioning of the monogamous family had been a common topic, much earlier, in the writings of Charles Fourier, one of the first socialists, who considered this type of family anti-natural, because it repressed passions—those linked to carnal love, as well as those of a platonic nature—and was grounded on the supposed inferiority of women. We should not forget that the condition of women in many of the communities built following the ideas of the first socialists was anything but enviable—there were fortunate exceptions, though, such as those associated with certain communities of an anarchist nature or with some, but not all, of the experiments encouraged by Owenists and Fourierists.[4] In general terms, it should be said that in this scenario a greater emphasis was placed on the practice of free love—regardless of what was understood by this concept—than on the liberation of women.

---

3 Waintrop, *Les anarchists espagnols*, 467–69.

4 See "La femme et la famille," in Jean-Christian Petitfils, *Les communautés utopistes au XIXe siècle* (Paris: Pluriel, 2011), 257–78.

Certainly, and as it would be expected, the majority of the contributions in this field came from libertarian women. The North American Voltairine de Cleyre, little known among us, defended free love and birth control, rejected monogamy and the grounds for the sexual division of labor, and condemned repeatedly the double exploitation suffered by women as a result. Louise Michel struggled against the discrimination suffered by women and for the equality of the sexes. The Argentine anarchist Carmen Lareva emphasized how inequality functioned to the detriment of women but not without forcefully denouncing sexual hypocrisy and the exploitation that characterize our societies. Emma Goldman, for her part, argued that the only difference between a married woman and a prostitute is the permanent character of exploitation suffered by the former, demanding the complete independence of women. The Spanish Teresa Claramunt and Teresa Mañé challenged the arguments sustaining the inherent superiority of men, a fictitious superiority that is, nonetheless, at the core of all social organization. Many of these ideas were at the origin of a movement called Mujeres Libres, very fertile in the 1930s. Thus, despite Federica Montseny's inclination to stress that anarchism had never "distinguished between man and woman,"[5] the daily reality of many of the anarchist organizations—and I had the opportunity to notice this—belied time and again the good intentions of such a statement. In the dense social magma in which contradictions were frequent, it is sufficient to recall that in the wake of the 1936 revolution, despite many anarchists and anarcho-syndicalists being firmly determined to close the brothels, there were others equally determined to defend their continuity under the singular argument that invoked the need for providing workers and militia men with an escape.[6]

5   Federica Montseny, quoted in Termes, *Història del movement anarquista a Espanya*, 618.

6   Ealham, *Anarchism and the City*, 189.

Nowadays it is a rather easy to discern a fluid relation between radical feminism and anarchism. Many libertarian feminists have underlined that, in actuality, the majority of radical feminists are unconsciously anarchists. Peggy Kornegger has stated, "Women's intuitive anarchism, if sharpened and clarified, is an incredible leap forward (or beyond) in the struggle for human liberation."[7] At the same time, in the libertarian world there is a strong conviction that strictly feminist organizations are necessary, in the same vein as *affinity groups*. In this respect, a necessity imposes itself of breaking with the isolation that so many women suffer and the enforced consciousness that they must liberate themselves, without reproducing schemas of domination and submission and on the basis of mutual aid, equality, and the refusal of leaderships. The emancipation of women will be the work of women themselves, or it will not be.

I am referring to an anarcho-feminism that openly contests capitalism, recalls that patriarchy and class exploitation maintain an obvious interrelation, and concerns itself with an extremely broad range of issues. This variety is illustrated in the critique of marriage and the nuclear family, heterosexuality's radical primacy, fixed sexual identities, hierarchical norms, alienating divisions, stereotypes expressed in education and culture, and a double exploitation. This is also confirmed by the desire to increase power over the body and the aspiration to reinvent everyday life. To demand equality between men and women in a system weighed down ontologically by inequality and hierarchy leads to a multitude of contradictions. Some problems are likely to resolve themselves but only at the cost of reinforcing others, in a theater where the evident risk of reproducing the rules of the game of power—at the origin of the marginalization of women—seems palpable. "Feminism doesn't mean female corporate power or a woman

---

7   Peggy Kornegger, in Dark Star, *Quiet Rumours: An Anarcha-Feminist Reader* (Oakland: AK Press, 2012), 31.

President; it means *no* corporate power and *no* Presidents."[8] Ultimately, what seems to reveal itself is a deep awareness regarding what power signifies: if it survives in a matriarchal society, many of the usual problems will survive as well. With such difficulties, it is not hard to understand how the critique of omnipresent state feminism has been strengthened, bound as it is to the idea that problems can be fully resolved by demanding an assortment of things from state institutions. And it is equally unsurprising that the rebellious potential of radical feminism's global discourse makes itself felt at times.

Biological Resistances

I have already noted that the ecological question does not have a very consistent presence in the writings of nineteenth-century anarchists. The only exception in this regard is perhaps expressed in the work of Élisée Reclus. Of course, some will say that circumstances were even more delicate back then. Kropotkin, to cite but one example, not only seemed to share with Marx the same certainties concerning the seemingly impossible exhaustion of natural resources but also disagreed harshly with the Luddites and criticized the antipathy that machinery provoked in William Morris, adhering, in turn, to the acritical praise of mechanization displayed at another time by William Godwin. Furthermore, some decades later, all of the currents of the Spanish libertarian world, from the *treintistas* to the *faístas*,[9] incautiously embraced a productivist perception that ingenuously idealized work and consumption.

Despite all of this, it is also true that an almost biological mistrust can be seen among the majority of anarchist

---

8   Ibid.

9   *Treintistas* and *faístas* was a distinction that emerged within the Spanish CNT in the early 1930s between a more reformist versus a more radical tendency within the union. [translator]

thinkers regarding the virtues, idolized by Marx, of large industrial complexes, of centralized mass production, and of
the strict regimentation of labor that took shape, for instance,
under Taylorism. The defense of self-management and direct
democracy constituted an interesting antidote to such projects and realities. This aside, and relatedly, not all anarchist
thinkers proposed societies marked by the desirability of
abundance. Thus, for example, the aforementioned Godwin,
for whom luxury was an inexorable source of corruption, advocated that one should work only enough to assure happi-
ness and affirmed that the simpler life is, the better. Austerity
and self-restraint were, in any case, part of the daily life of
militants and libertarian organizations. It is enough to recall
the example of many Spanish anarchist peasants who clearly
struggled for a simple and austere life.

Another mental paradigm that forcefully contributed—
and still does—to protecting what should be understood
as a spontaneous ecological consciousness in the libertarian
world was the aim of defending many of the organizational
and relational habits of *primitive societies*.[10] Studies like those
carried out by Sahlins, Clastres, or Zerzan—which I have
mentioned above—have served to identify societies based on
mutual aid, both in the past as well as in the present, that
are not subject to the logic of accumulation and profit and
are neither hierarchized nor burdened by the institution of
the state. I believe that the paradigm that I refer to has rarely
led to any naive analyses but has rather helped to distinguish
healthy elements in human communities that otherwise present very divergent perspectives.

This sort of biological defense that libertarian thought has
been able to exhibit, together with recent efforts to deepen
inquiries into the significance of the ecological crisis, makes
pathetic the claims, so often repeated in the past, that suggest

---

10 See Beltrán Roca, ed., *Anarquismo y antropología* (Madrid: La
   Malatesta, 2008).

that anarchism is a worldview completely unsuited to the challenges of complex societies. Let us consider, for instance, this claim of paradoxical naïveté by Irving Lewis Horowitz: "It scarcely requires any feats of mind to show that modern industrial life is incompatible with the anarchist demand for the liquidation of state authority."[11] The answer is simple: the incompatibility is welcome, because thanks to it, anarchism continues to be fully relevant today, inasmuch as it appears recalcitrant and dedicated to contesting the supposed virtues of complex societies.

Degrow, Deurbanize, Detechnologize, Decomplexify

In my opinion, there are four verbs, as it were, that enable libertarian thought when it comes to confronting the ecological crisis and its challenges: degrow, deurbanize, detechnologize, and decomplexify.

The term we employ to capture the corresponding project is of little importance. What I usually call *degrowth* is based on the certainty that, if we live on a planet with limited resources, it is senseless that we aspire to grow without limit, especially when there are more than enough reasons to be suspicious of growth's supposed positive effects. In regard to the countries of the opulent global North, the need arises, therefore, of considerably reducing the economic activity of those areas that are at the center of the uncontrolled expansion of the ecological footprint. Over time, then, a number of explicit demands takes shape: the recuperation of the social life that we have been losing, the organization of creative forms of leisure, the sharing of work, the dimensional reduction of many of the infrastructures that we use, the recuperation of local life—in a setting of reemerging direct democracy and self-management—and, at the individual level, a voluntary simplicity and sobriety. It is important to remember

11 Irving Lewis Horowitz, quoted in Price, *The Abolition of the State*, 80.

that degrowth is not a worldview that acts as a substitute for older forms of challenges to capitalism that we have known for a long time. Rather, it is proposed in addition to these challenges. An essential addition, though: whenever I have had the opportunity, I have emphasized that any opposition to capitalism in the opulent world at the beginnings of the twenty-first century has to be, by definition, against growth and patriarchy, internationalist, and advocating self-management; otherwise, it will unequivocally be turning the gears of the very system it pretends to oppose.

It seems easier to explain what should be understood by *deurbanizing*. The last hundred years of a society like ours have been characterized by a dramatic venture of deruralization, a process as essential as it is forgotten: rural life moribund, many elements of popular wisdom and many forms of organization, which feel critical to avoiding or at least mitigating the looming collapse, have disappeared. In turn, we have inherited visibly overdimensioned and uninhabitable cities, which emphatically reveal—and it is already here—an opposing movement of city inhabitants who seek to return to a rural environment.. When we speak of the creation of self-managed and decommodified spaces of autonomy, the greater part of our attention is forcefully directed toward their development in this domain.

I willingly assume that *detechnologizing* involves a certain degree of provocation. Contemporary libertarians are accustomed to pairing a frequent and consistent use of technology—computer science above all else—with a critical discourse in regard to that same technology, something that is not without its contradictions. John Zerzan, an essayist I have mentioned on several occasions, has made a radical critique of all technologies created under capitalism.[12] From

---

12 John Zerzan (ed.), *Against Civilization* (Los Angeles: Feral House, 2005); John Zerzan, *Twilight of the Machines* (Port Townsend: Feral House, 2008).

his perspective, which merits attention, these technologies always bear the mark of exploitation, of division of labor and hierarchy, in such a way that it is very difficult to see how they could be a contributing factor in any emancipatory project. Without going any further, the mistrust toward the many technologies imposed on us and naively employed by us as if they were strictly neutral is more than justified. And this seems more evident when there is no reason to conclude that these technologies may by themselves engender self-management or the reconstruction of a lost social life, and when data accumulates that lead us to consider that many of these technologies reveal desire to permanently surveil and control. Did the absence of contemporary means of communication prevent, by the way, the actions of the CNT in the 1930s? Were not these actions, technologically poor, much more efficient than the bureaucratic machinery of today?

I will finish with *decomplexification*. There are more than enough reasons to state that we are ever more dependent because we have accepted societies that are ever more complex. Therefore, if we wish to recover independence, we will necessarily have to reduce the complexity of the environments in which we live. Many of the disinherited of the world, inhabitants of the countries of the global South, find themselves paradoxically in a better position than ours to face the likely coming collapse: they live in small human communities, have maintained a much richer social life than is evident in our cities, have preserved a much more fluid relation with the natural world, and, as I have just suggested, they are much more independent. Let us imagine what would happen in any of the opulent societies should the supplies of oil ceased flowing in: their whole fragile edifice would crumble overnight, a circumstance that by itself obliges us to conclude that it is much more advantageous to bet on human communities that, in the face of complexity and personal hedonistic gratification, call for self-restraint, simplicity, equality, solidarity, and horizontalism. Besides, the material conditions for direct democracy necessarily call for less complex societies and smaller communities.

Bookchin's Polemic

One of the most controversial texts of recent years in the libertarian world bears the title *Social Anarchism or Lifestyle Anarchism.*[13] Its author, Murray Bookchin, now deceased, was a very well-known polemicist who had the virtue of recovering, from an anarchist perspective, central debates associated with, for example, ecology or libertarian municipalism.

I suspect that a good part of the controversy generated by Bookchin's little book has to do with the fact that it is difficult not to feel sympathy for the arguments raised therein. Bookchin defends, and rightfully so, a *social* and combative anarchism, one with a class consciousness and an emphatically altruistic vocation. From this perspective, he criticizes—often in a thought-provoking manner—countercultural and individualist anarchism, anarcho-primitivism, neo-Luddism, and many of the contemporary challenges to technology. All in all, Bookchin understands that this whole hodgepodge of views can be summarized by the following traits: "Ad hoc adventurism, personal bravura, an aversion to theory oddly akin to the antirational biases of postmodernism, celebrations of theoretical incoherence (pluralism), a basically apolitical and anti-organizational commitment to imagination, desire, and ecstasy, and an intensely self-oriented enchantment of everyday life."[14] When it is not—I shall add—witchcraft and mysticism.

---

13 Murray Bookchin, *Social Anarchism or Lifestyle Anarchism: An Unbridgeable Chasm* (Oakland: AK Press, 1995).

14 Ibid., 9. A good example of the texts criticized by Bookchin is the hardly understandable little book by Hakim Bey, *T.A.Z.: The Temporary Autonomous Zone* (New York: Autonomedia, 2003).

For me, as for many others, it appears that Bookchin's analysis is sketched too roughly. A clear defense of *social* and combative anarchism notwithstanding, we should nevertheless avoid, for instance, the quick dismissal of counterculture contributions. Let us not forget, to name but one fact, that counterculture has put forward an necessary critique of prudish and bourgeois puritanism, a critique that also obliges one to keep a distance from the propagandist simplicity of many versions of classical anarchism, often very close to socialist realism and its weaknesses. We only need to take a glimpse at the films made by the CNT in the 1930s or the many texts published in *La Novela Ideal*: "The heroes appear sublime, they are altruistic and display solidarity, and they confront negative elements, generally isolated and often distant from the people. The principal protagonists are usually men, and women assume a much more passive role."[15] The same can be said of anarcho-primitivism, which—whatever its distortions and simplifications—raises a necessary discussion with regard to complex societies, technology, or cities. Ultimately, it is one thing is to struggle to limit hedonistic tendencies in order to the rights of others, and a very different one to eradicate these tendencies by bowing to a moral code that invokes intolerance and inquisitions.

In another domain, it is evident that Bookchin naively idealizes the emancipatory potential of technologies. To confer a social dimension upon the analyses of the latter does not magically solve the problem, nor does it convert those technologies into instruments of emancipation or cancel their frequent ties to division of labor, exploitation, and alienation. To forget social relations and conditions under capitalism and to idealize the benefits of the technologies rendered possible by it is problematic. And Bookchin does not seem to realize this, however much he sometimes also flirts with a radical critique of technological knowledge. His much more frequent aim of

---

15 Termes, *Història del movement anarquista a Espanya*, 386.

separating himself from technology's radical critics provokes in most cases, and in other words, a censorship that cancels out any good intentions. Doing away with capitalism will not, by itself, free us from many of the effects of inherited technologies. Also, Bookchin does not show himself prone to appreciating—and this is perhaps more serious—many of the problems that accompany societies *of abundance*.

In conclusion, if we approved of what Bookchin advocates in the cited work, anarchism would have fallen behind other worldviews in terms of lucidity. Fortunately and obviously, we are not obliged to accept the arguments of our author. And it seems more reasonable that we seek to build bridges here, as in so many other areas, between currents, movements, and generations. This extends also to counterculture, anarcho-primitivism, and neo-Luddism.

Terminal Decay and Collapse

Over the last few years, I have often reiterated that we have become overly accustomed to using the word *crisis* in the singular to identify the cadence of a phenomenon the system has decided to denominate as *financial*, when we far too frequently forget that other crises—in plural—are at work behind the scenes. I am thinking of climate change, which is a disquieting reality that is already here and that has no positive consequences whatsoever; the inevitable increase, in the medium and long term, in the prices of the majority of primary energy resources that we use; the demographic problems that beset many of the regions of the planet; the condition of deep submission that so many women suffer; or, simply, the pursuit of exploitation of human and material wealth in the countries of the global South. If each of these crises taken separately is worrying enough, their combination is literally explosive. Let us not forget, however, that the very concept of *crisis* is in large part a Western product: it can only be explained if, within the framework of a cyclical vision of events, periods of prosperity and recession are identifiable, which hardly occurs in the global South. I recall that many years ago, when I asked a Uruguayan colleague how they endured the country's uncontrolled inflation, he replied with a fortunate sense of humor: "Here in Uruguay we live in a state of balanced bankruptcy." Thus, it is important to take into consideration the effects of past colonialism, including those that influence the concepts that we employ, and to act accordingly.

There are sound reasons to argue that capitalism has entered a phase of terminal corrosion. Capitalism is a system that historically has demonstrated a formidable capacity to adapt to the most diverse of challenges. The great debate today refers to whether or not capitalism is dramatically losing the braking mechanisms that have allowed it to save face in the past. In other words, if—driven by a seemingly unstoppable impulse, bent on the accumulation of spectacular profits in a very short period of time—it is not simultaneously digging its own grave, with the additional complication that it may very well collapse on our heads. Although capitalism has always been a system of exploitation, unjust and excluding, we have to agree that it has also been a reasonably efficient formula: it assured that the majority of business people gained the profits that they competed for. This cannot be witnessed today, in a scenario in which many of the apologists for the neoliberal project, having rejected any type of intervention in the economy by public authorities, have quickly come to demand from the government—in what amounts to a greater sign of ineffectiveness—the assistance necessary for the salvation of their businesses. There is also no discernible will to reform on the part of capitalism, or any kind of awareness of the dangers that threaten. This is particularly surprising when it comes to the enormous effects of the ecological crisis in its dual nature: the irreversible environmental aggressions and the exhaustion of basic resources that seriously imperil the rights of future generations and, with them, that of other species that accompany us on this planet. What is in crisis is not unregulated capitalism, as our latest social democrats pretend, but rather capitalism itself.

Yet it is important to attend to the possible manifestations of what some pundits begin to call *ecofascism*. In a highly recommendable book, *Hitler als Vorläufer: Auschwitz-der Beginn des 21. Jahrhunderts*, author Carl Amery develops an evocative thesis.[16] We would be very much mistaken— he tells us—if we believed that the policies embraced by the German Nazis eighty years ago were the product of a circumstantial and unique historical moment and, therefore, fortunately unrepeatable. Amery rather exhorts us to thoroughly examine the actual content of these policies and to do so for a specific reason: these may well reappear in the upcoming years—this time, however, not supported by ultra-marginal neo-Nazi groups but rather put forward by the principal centers of political and economic power, ever more conscious of the looming general scarcity and more firmly determined to preserve these scarce resources in the hands of a few by virtue of a project of *militarized social Darwinism*. We should seriously consider whether many of the Western leaders' gambles do not sink their roots in a project of this nature or at least lean in that direction. And let us admit, indeed, that ecofascism may be capitalism's incipient response to the terminal corrosion referred to above, and with it, to the concomitant collapse.

Pacifism, Antimilitarism, Violence

I have already mentioned that, in contrast to what occurred with the stories of feminism and environmentalism, pacifist and antimilitarist struggles have always had a significant presence in libertarian thought. I will first refrain from making

---

16 Carl Amery, *Hitler als Vorläufer: Auschwitz-der Beginn des 21. Jahrhunderts* (München: Luchterhand, 1998) [*Auschwitz, ¿comienza el siglo XXI? Hitler como precursor* (Madrid: Turner, 2002).]

any distinctions between these two, often different, positions. I will rather limit myself to stating that it would certainly be erroneous to conclude that these two struggles have lost momentum and interest. Today the military apparatus—so apparently and self-interestedly humanized—continues to invade everything, without anything basic having changed. The Israeli model can serve as testimony to demonstrate that the rules of representative democracy are compatible with *apartheid* and, in their case, with genocide. Yet we can also find cases of the repressive-military utilization of emergency situations (and, with them, of *natural* disasters), the establishment of the myth of *humanitarian intervention*, the planetary expansion of the military industrial complex, and the refinement of elaborated strategies of intimidation toward citizens. Let us consider, both in the Spanish case and in relation to all these questions, the work and implications of the so-called Unidad Militar de Emergencias (Military Emergencies Unit), which is directed toward preparing the population for the active presence of the armed forces in the most diverse of circumstances.

However it must be highlighted that a good part of the disputes that to a greater or lesser extent have a presence in pacifist and antimilitarist debates, refers to the eternal question of violence—a well-known question that has given rise to deep divisions among libertarians. There are many pacifist anarchists, and there are many pacifists who consider themselves anarchists: both have defended passive resistance and nonviolent direct action. Yet it is also true that the idea that they are pacifists in no way pleases many anarchists.[17] For the latter, it is easy to see the concept of pacifism as a way of acting that is only within the reach of a minority of the population in very select countries, whereas, in the overwhelming majority of cases, the scenario doubtless compels us to assume positions that are, in one way or another, violent.[18] Nor

---

17 Graeber, *Direct Action*, 224.

18 Ibid., 225.

is there any shortage of those who say that they believe in the armed struggle, without ever venturing to practice it, and, even more, who confess in public their commitment to it—a circumstance that obliges us to reflect on the mental stability of such individuals.

Despite the way it has been branded, the libertarian movement has shown itself to be far less violent than others. One only has to think of the background of fascism, colonizing liberalism, barracks communism, certain manifestations of nationalism, many religious beliefs, or the great powers. Anarchists have never engaged in massive and indiscriminate forms of violence. While none of the libertarian thinkers—not even Bakunin—have uncritically defended violence, many of them, albeit cautiously, have displayed a clear awareness of the shortcomings and problems that come with it. Kropotkin argued, "Of all parties I now see only one party—the Anarchist—which respects human life, and loudly insists upon the abolition of capital punishment, prison torture and punishment of man by man altogether. All other parties teach every day their utter disrespect of human life."[19] Against this backdrop, we find the violence of the system, the violence that generally escapes the attention of our disinformation media: the violence of many businesspeople over their workers, of so many men over women, the one exercised by the police against the undocumented, the one that all of us deploy against the natural environment, or, certainly, the violence of genuine wars of plunder. One does not have to be terribly astute to realize that behind all of this evidently lies the state, the principal agent of violence, so brilliantly revealed by Tolstoy. Violence is inherent to the state.

In a text that cannot but be controversial, but which in any case possesses a pedagogical virtue, David Graeber invites us to bring some order to the libertarian debate on violence.[20]

---

19 Peter Kropotkin, quoted in Marshall, *Demanding the Impossible*, 633.

20 Graeber, *Direct Action*, 222ff.

In this regard, he has initially identified various reasons for its rejection. One of these reasons states that if an anarchist must act in conformity with the values of the society that she wishes to create, with violence logically not among them, then it is up to her to reject violence. Furthermore, to be efficient, the latter calls for hierarchical structures that do sit well with the libertarian worldview; therefore, by requiring clandestine and secret conduct, violence renders difficult the parallel realization of genuinely democratic principles. I would say that violence may also go hand in hand with an extremely poor evaluation of its consequences, and it may also ruin any prospects of genuine mass movements. Thus, Graeber notes that there is a compelling reason to justify a prudent acceptance of violence: the proposed social revolution is difficult to imagine without the use of violence to one degree or another. The American libertarian addresses several delicate issues, such as the need to determine what is understood by violence or when it assumes gratuitous forms devoid of any purpose—beyond self-satisfaction or a misconceived aesthetic—and without any collective project on the back burner, as was exemplified by many anarchists responsible for attacks during the nineteenth and twentieth centuries. Although many libertarians have asked themselves whether it was reasonable to criticize the violence committed against political leaders or economic magnates responsible for the misery and exploitation of many, others have shown concern for a tarnished image, detrimental to anarchist movements and a direct result of arbitrary violence. Yet many others have also underscored the fact that these movements' demonization would take place with or without the use of violence.

VIII.

NATIONS, SOUTHERN ANARCHISMS

The National Question and Anarchism

SOME MONTHS AGO, the publication of one of the anarcho-syndicalist forces active among us expressed an idea that was not without significance. Referring to the period prior to the Spanish Civil War, it stated that "the anarchists were not separatists." Few terrains have been as muddy as the one concerning anarchism and the national question. "How could an anarchist be a nationalist?," ask those who sometimes find themselves fully immersed, perhaps unknowingly, in the logic of state nationalism. How could anarchists distance themselves—others inquire—from a national question that is at the core of many of the disputes relative to state formation and its democratic nature?

At some point in the past, I suggested that there are only two reasonable ways to address the national question. The first one states that, since the nineteenth century and on a significant part of the planet, political communities articulate themselves unequivocally and unavoidably in the form of nations that are, to borrow Benedict Anderson's expression, *imagined communities*, whereas the second considers nations to be artificial and vested constructs that respond to the brazen aim of setting aside the class struggle and assuring the corresponding privileges of the bourgeoisies. On paper, the latter would have been the overwhelmingly dominant view held by the libertarian movement, and as a result it would have extricated itself from the quite bitter disputes and positions crystallized by the national question.

I am afraid that the facts concerning the libertarian perspective are nonetheless more complex. I shall simply stress that there are anarchist thinkers—Bakunin, for instance—who see in nations a natural, or almost natural, fact, which is not in itself seen as an obstacle to the necessarily universalist and internationalist character of the libertarian project. "As a Slav, I wanted the liberation of the Slav race from the German yoke. I wanted this liberation to be brought about by the revolution, that is to say by the destruction of the regime of Russia, Austria, Prussia, and Turkey, and by the reorganization of the peoples from below upwards through their own freedom, upon the foundation of complete economic and social equality, and not through the power of any authority, however revolutionary it might call itself, and however intelligent it might in fact be," wrote the celebrated author.[1] One of the recurrent elements in the Russian anarchist's oeuvre, however, is the idea that social revolution is intrinsic to the liberation of subjected peoples. Certainly, far from proposing a kind of nationalism longed for by the state, Bakunin advocated a very different horizon, one that was grounded in a revolutionary and federalist project.

1   Mikhail Bakunin, quoted in Lehning, *Conversaciones con Bakunin*, 102.

Yet, if we follow the views that I have just summarized, we would fail to do justice to reality by stating that, from a libertarian perspective, *internationalism* and *nationalism* are diametrically opposing phenomena.

On the other hand, there is no disagreement among anarchist thinkers in regard to a critique of a characteristic that permeates the vast majority of manifestations of nationalism, one that attributes to them an omnipresent statist desire that reveals itself with particular force, of course, in *state* nationalisms—an argument that was strenuously expressed by Rudolf Rocker in *Nationalism and Culture.*[2] At the same time that strong criticisms stand out, once more, against nationalism as an interclassist phenomenon, a suspicious distinction appears, which separates oppressive nations from oppressed nations, seemingly ignoring the fact that in each of these supposed instances there are very different realities and, hence, very different classes.

Although in libertarian thought it is uncommon to forget the ascendancy of state nationalisms—those silent nationalisms that would seem not to exist—I must admit that there have certainly been problems in this regard. In the pre-1939 Catalan libertarian world, there were frequent disputes with many immigrant workers who seemed not to accept in any way the culture and the language of the country where they had arrived. On the other hand, the libertarian movement has quite often accepted organizational formulas that copied the institutional-administrative framework of the state to a considerable degree, with no desire to discuss them. We may find palpable traces of this in the *National* Confederation of Labor or in the different *regional* committees. Moreover, it was unclear whether the defense of an *Iberian* project would have resolved this confusion, for the formula in question implied the acceptance of an entity configured by two states,

---

2   Rudolf Rocker, *Nationalism and Culture* (Montreal: Black Rose Books, 1998).

often permeated, by the way, by imperial connotations. Indeed, yet contrary to this argument, it has always been facile to appreciate a very close relation between the Catalan libertarian movement and the corresponding national demand. A stronger relation, though, occurs in the case of anarcho-syndicalism and especially in its syndicalist elements—a phenomenon that is well illustrated in the book by Termes that I have cited a number of times.

If I must express my convictions—which are very close to those included in the collective book *Anarquisme i alliberament nacional*—in regard to how to best address the national question from a libertarian perspective, I would say, first and foremost, that it seems unwise to ignore what it signifies, which in no way implies accepting that the nationalist proposition is the master formula for confronting the issue (it surely seems wise to clarify beforehand what should be understood by nationalism).[3] Second, I would suggest that, when dealing with such issues, it is necessary to heed the development and actions of state nationalisms, given that otherwise it is very easy for dramatic distortions of complex realities to take place. Third, I shall argue that it is suitable to separate the terms *nationalism* and *independence*. Upholding the latter does not need to translate into a parallel defense of state formation and the creation of an army. Independence should arise from the accumulation of previous independences coming from below: the individual, the communal, the regional, et cetera, since—we must assume—it is essential to liberate oneself from oppressions. This is what it logically means to gain independence. I would also like to underscore my boundless suspicion of all macrostructures that capital has been shaping—the European Union, for instance—an open contradiction to the perception of those who only see advantages in bottom-up integration.

---

3   Ricard de Vargas-Golarons et al., *Anarquisme i alliberament nacional* (Barcelona: Catarko/La Ciutat Invisible/Collectiu Negres Tempestes/ Virus, 2007).

And I shall add, finally, that whatever the excesses surrounding the principle of self-determination and its corresponding laws, both of them are preferable to their negation, unless, of course, we declare ourselves proudly hostile to the cause of democracy and thoroughly defend actually existing states.

Anarchism in the Global South

I feel obliged to offer some notes on a discussion that, though rare, is nevertheless important: is not anarchism perhaps—despite its emancipatory pretentions—just another expression of a clearly Eurocentric perception that reproduces to perfection this perspective and is thus incapable of travelling across borders, or, when it does, transferring codes and ways of acting that are exclusive to the geographical areas from which it originates?

It would be absurd to deny any significance to this question and assume that a negative answer to it resolves the matter. That such Eurocentric and ultimately colonial spasms have been able to manifest themselves at some point seems beyond discussion. Yet three responses can be formulated. The first one stresses anarchism's permanent commitment to contesting colonizations and imperialisms: as Anderson has revealed, anticolonial discourse has always had a consistent presence in libertarian thought.[4] I shall admit, however, that anarchism's relation with colonial contestation is one thing, and the actual deployment of anarchism in the affected countries during and after colonization is another.

I believe nonetheless that we would be shutting our eyes to reality—and this is the second response—if we forgot about the presence of movements of a strictly anarchist nature in the countries of the global South. It is worth mentioning the names of China—where in the past there was a significant

---

4   Benedict Anderson, *Under Three Flags: Anarchism and the Anti-Colonial Imagination* (London: Verso, 2005).

anarchist movement—or Palestine or India—two places where a libertarian presence continues to make itself felt—or, of course, Latin America, where the waves of Spanish, Portuguese, and Italian migrations consequently had and still have a notable influence on libertarian organizations.[5]

A third and last response can be put forth, something that places us in an order of events that differs from what has so far concerned us here; that is, a response that recalls the obvious existence of libertarian practices—I choose this adjective for it is clearly more appropriate—in many human communities of the global South. It is certainly not a case of mimetic imitations of northern anarchists' demands. Rather, I speak of communities that exude a libertarian way of life and that challenge Western values and the logic of colonization. Such is the case, for example, of African communalism or the many indigenous peoples of Latin America;, human communities that, by the way, do not always adjust themselves to the particular stereotype forged in the heat of anarcho-primitivism, which in some cases, and contrary to appearances, is nothing more than the expression of perceptions rooted in the opulent global North and its own rules of the game. And it is clear that these communities' condition owes nothing to the enlightened preconceptions that have inspired classical anarchism, all the more so when these preconceptions frequently respond to much more diffuse conceptions of class.[6] However, this situation obliges us to acknowledge that, on many occasions, strictly anarchist movements based in the countries of the global South, bent on reproducing an ideological canon stemming from the global North, have followed paths very different from those marked by the fundamentally libertarian practices of a large part of these countries' native inhabitants.

---

5   See Barret, *Los sediciosos despertares de la anarquía.*

6   Sharif Gemie, in Graham, *A Documentary History of Libertarian Ideas, Volume 3,* 324.

CONCLUSION

I want to underscore several characteristics of the libertarian worldview. The first is the profoundly rooted awareness that we are part of the same system that we wish to bring down. This awareness outlines, I believe, a fundamental difference in regard to the habits of the *traditional left*, comfortably established under the idea that everything, or almost everything, is reducible to a confrontation between the good and the lucid, on the one hand, and the bad and the wicked, on the other. Decades ago, with a language that is no longer current, Cornelius Castoriadis referred to the constant rebirth of capitalist reality at the heart of the proletariat. Steve Biko, with the same insistence, noticed that "the most potent weapon in the hands of the oppressor is the mind of the oppressed."[1]

Another important characteristic that has already called my attention on more than one occasion in this text is that, in my opinion, the libertarian world should hold on to the steadfast aim of rejecting calls for purity and self-centered group realities in favor of working with common people. It would be bad if the discourse of contemporary anarchism

---

1   Steve Biko, *I Write What I Like: Selected Writings*, ed. Aelred Stubbs (Chicago: University of Chicago Press, 2002), 92.

were reduced to that of a closed identitarian group; rather, it should always open itself onto popular struggles, immersed in the great flows of contestation and emancipation, in a free dialogue with other currents. Holloway has emphasized that it is not a matter of everyone being a radical anti-capitalist: what happens is that the experience of capitalist oppression generates in many people the beginning of a rejection and rebellion that should be stimulated.[2] Therefore, there is no artificial creation of a consciousness or an outside leadership but rather the recovery of something that is already there. No revolution can be carried out—as Lenin pretends—in the name of others. For Lenin, the workers are by themselves incapable of transcending the world of superficial trade union consciousness, and thus it is necessary to push their consciousness from the outside, by those who possess a social science that provides certainties; that is to say, by those who belong to the educated higher classes. Holloway states that "scientific socialism … is the theory of the emancipation of the proletariat, but certainly not of its self-emancipation."[3] As a result, a separation arises between a *them*—the proletariat—and an *us*—the people, bearers of consciousness, who should take over power in the name of others.

I would add that this desire to accompany the common people should clearly be expressed with modesty. Outbursts of superiority and self-conscious certainties have always provided bad counsel. It would be unfortunate if we, with fierce determination, set out to demonize rather than appeal to others, which is something that tends to occur quite often. "Beware of believing anarchy to be a dogma, a doctrine above question or debate, to be venerated by its adepts as is the Koran by devout Moslems. No! The absolute freedom which we demand constantly develops our thinking and raises it toward new horizons (according to the turn of mind of various

2   Holloway, *Change the World without Taking Power*, 226.

3   Ibid., 130.

individuals), takes it out of the narrow framework of regulation and codification. We are not 'believers'!," stated Émile Henry just before being sent to the guillotine.[4]

This does not mean that we should close our eyes and mouths before unedifying realities. We must certainly be suspicious of an anarchism this is mere graffiti and easy gestures, oblivious to self-management and direct action. For there indeed exists an anarchism of appearances and external signs, very radical in its expressions, but which is often detached from any transformative practices. If this kind of anarchism deserves a consistent critique, then it would not be appropriate for us to consider the hardened and organic militancy of yore to be flawless either. Not to mention that—given a choice—maximalism is much more useful than possibilism, which seems to permeate everything.

Even so, we should keep our distance from those dogmatic and pure anarchists who never dirty their hands. "Sitting, waiting for the revolution, / The chair, my boss lent it to me," goes a song by Sérgio Godinho. It is very easy to write radical accusations against the state and no less radical defenses of libertarian communism without feeling the obligation to think through what we should and can do right now. The perception of many complex situations is inevitably different for those who struggle and for those who limit themselves to reflection. If we add a very delicate phenomenon—the haughty disdain of those presumed ignorant or inept—the circle closes dangerously. This is particularly the case when the protagonists of such conduct display a special and pathological interest in seeking out enemies within the very libertarian world, as if they attempted to give shape to a space from which all *competitors* ought to disappear completely. It is unsurprising that all those who behave in this way tend to reproduce all the habits of an obstinate and blind (*zorrocotroco*) world that blossomed a long time ago in the *traditional*

---

4   Émile Henry, quoted in Guérin, *Anarchism*, 3–4.

left. The drivel about revealed truths and rapturous working classes may well measure up to those announced with great assurance by Leninist, Trotskyist, and Stalinist sects, through organizations and personalities that possess a facade of activism but no reality behind them. Radicalism should be acknowledged, provided that it does not become a theater of appearances, paradoxically useful to power. We are already familiar enough with those who have dogmatically defended anarchist purity and who ultimately walked off toward other horizons. For, in the end, it is very hard to remain pure for any period of time.

I return, in closing, to a subject that I pointed out in the prologue of this book: there are enough reasons to conclude that the libertarian project has more weight and meaning today than ever before. In the eyes of more and more people, it seems clear that we should contest all powers, especially those enforced by capitalism and the state. We should do this, moreover, from the perspective of leaderless organizations where self-management and direct action are given priority, while simultaneously ascribing equal importance to the rights of women, of future generations, and of the afflicted inhabitants of the countries of the global South. To the logic of private profit and accumulation, we should oppose the logic of solidarity, mutual aid, and restraint, in a scenario marked by a double consciousness: that we are not without our limitations and that we are part of the very system we want to bring down. I would like to close this book with a quote by Emma Goldman that I included in the final pages of the anthology of libertarian thinkers that I published in 2010. It reads: "I consider Anarchism the most beautiful and practical philosophy that has yet been thought of in its application to individual expression and the relation it establishes between the individual and society. Moreover, I am certain that Anarchism is too vital and too close to human nature ever to die. It is my conviction that dictatorship, whether to the right or to the left, can never work—that it never has worked, and that time will prove this again, as it has been proved before. When the failure of modern dictatorship and authoritarian philosophies becomes more apparent and the realization of failure more general, Anarchism will be vindicated. Considered from this point, a recrudescence of Anarchist ideas in the near future is very probable. When this occurs and takes effect, I believe that humanity will at last leave the maze in which it is now lost and will start on the path to sane living and regeneration through freedom."[5]

---

5 Emma Goldman, "A Life Worth Living," in Robert Graham (ed.), *Anarchism: A Documentary History of Libertarian Ideas, Volume 1: From Anarchy to Anarchism (300 CE to 1939)* (Montreal: Black Rose Books, 2005), 496.

epilogue for this new edition:
RECENT DEVELOPMENTS

THE BOOK THE reader has in her hands is the third edition of *Rethinking Anarchy*. Should the circumstances have been different, it is very likely that a new prologue or epilogue would not have been necessary. But our current state of affairs seems to impose a reflective exercise in this regard, which may look extremely peculiar and stimulating for some, whereas for others—among which I am a part—it may take on a repetitive air of what we have already seen a thousand times before through the parliamentary illusion, the ballot box, political parties, and state institutions.

Before delving into this reflective exercise, however, another relative element comes to our attention, something which ought to worry us indeed: the fickle reaction that this new scenario seems to have provoked in the *libertarian* milieu, defined to some degree by the proliferation of labels that conspicuously use the first-person plural. To be honest, it is not very important if libertarians are happy to repeat, with or without reason, that what these labels carry is just a brief bloom, such that sooner or later we will have to stop taking heed of them. Yet many individuals—or perhaps, not that many—who claimed to be libertarian and continue to define themselves as such, seem bewitched today by a horizon of "real change" that involves the competitiveness of traditional ways of doing politics and that undoubtedly translates into strengthening the role of institutions. Furthermore, they brazenly spew the same arguments against the libertarian milieu that they themselves received for many years, if not decades.

In such a scenario, it is of utmost importance to acknowledge that, in order to defend our convictions with any shred of credibility, we should clean up our own house first. And this cleaning operation demands above all the identification of a bubble in which many of us have lived during the last few years. This bubble was birthed in May 2011 from a miscalculation, which led us to infer that we had reached the end of party politics, separation, and personalities for a new, advantageous era where self-organization, self-management, and direct democracy would take the helm. We must admit that the 15-M movement legitimately fed this conclusion, and what took place in recent months—namely, the controversial electoral results of Podemos and expectations that accompanied them—obliges us to state that the fruit was not as ripe as many of us thought.[1] By this I do not mean to show any inclination whatsoever toward belittling the overarching spirit of the 15-M movement: I still believe that it has been the best thing that has happened to us in a very long time,

---

1   Podemos is a political party that took advantage of—or co-opted—the energies and terminology of the leaderless, decentralized 15-M anti-austerity movement in Spain. [editor]

just as I still believe that we will have to adamantly debate what this implies or else invent something similar.

1.

A few weeks ago, at an alternative radio station, I was asked if there was any tinge of libertarianism in Podemos's approach. The answer is simple—absolutely not. Let us be clear about one thing: those responsible for this political force do not flirt, not even rhetorically, with any libertarian realm whatsoever. And they do not do so, first of all, because their short-term goal does not break in any way the mold of the social democratic creed, does not propose any new horizon to overcome capitalism, and does not care about capitalism's terminal corrosion or the impending collapse. Podemos's meandering is, moreover, that of a *catch all* party that, in hopes of widening its electoral support, does not think twice in defending the armed forces—guarantors of sovereignty—assuming a national-patriotic discourse, and avoiding ideological definitions, the same thing that the Partido Socialista Obrero Español (PSOE—Spanish Socialist Workers' Party) ended up doing in 1982.

The resulting project, directed by a hierarchical leadership, is based on what seems to be a fiction of assembly-like participation, very well-suited to the tastes of many of its supporters—some of whom are Facebook activists—and consistent with the acceptance of the miseries linked to elections, parliaments, and institutions. This picture is completed with the understanding that the illusions Podemos instills in people includes a troubling social and labor demobilization. Even though the responsibility for this does not belong exclusively to the new political force, it is surprising that its leaders do not seem particularly worried by it. This closeness to the institutions and this disdain for mobilizations and for the struggle are perhaps due to Podemos's belief that social movements are mere springs at the service of a project dictated by an omniscient vanguard, in a scenario that cannot be further away from what the word *self-management* means. I'm also very much afraid that Podemos's leaders, who think they are at the head of a process that's under their control, can very well be hostages to someone else's project.

Therefore, I will simply argue that Podemos is a burning nail from which many will have to tear themselves sooner or later. Those who favor the idea that today's tactical options will open the road of tomorrow to a more ambitious program seem to have misunderstood some basic facts. While, on the one hand, it is difficult to assert that they are not promoting a repetition of what we have already experienced in regard to the social and popular parties—the alarming distance between what they promise and what they actually do—on the other hand, they seem prone to ignore that there are no examples that give substance to this assumption of a drastic change toward the left in programs and practices. Yet I sense they are dodging a core issue: if the purpose of those responsible for Podemos is the one I'm defining here, their undeniable tactical talent would be countered by an amazing strategic ingenuity, which ignores that the sort of capitalism consummated in the European Union has already established a set of mandatory rules (and prescriptive punishments) for those who abide by the institutional game.

I start from the premise that the institutions and mainly the state are not there to serve whoever wishes to make use of them for whatever projects, even if those projects do not address anything more than a discourse—let us be generous—against the regime; that is, against the two-party system and corruption, while clearly forgetting the issues revolving around the system. The caste discourse is easily shared by those who fully defend the system. Among them, there are many businessmen who, biologically immersed in the liberal creed, are not keen on paying taxes, benefitting a parasitic and corrupt group of humans. If such a discourse is not coupled with an effective critique of capitalism and its derivatives, both in words and deeds, it can very well be that what remains is not simply the strategy of a catch all party but a project whose calling is to make the last turn of the screw in defense of the system. I will only point out in this respect that some of the champions of the system have begun to appreciate the deliberate ambiguity of Podemos concerning the sovereign process in Catalonia. Here I resort to a symbolically interesting example: it is the shot in the arm the Spanish state needs in this showdown. Why shouldn't we generalize the example to get a feel of what it would mean in other instances?

2.

The municipalist options are something completely different, which in many places take up the generic name of *Ganemos*.[2] In several cases, there are individuals with years of experience working in the autonomous world and social movements. To the assertion that municipalism possesses a clear libertarian inclination it is best to reply with a platitude: libertarian municipalism has a deep libertarian root, but applying this adjective to any municipalist perspective is erroneous at best. What the libertarian world has always defended is the free, self-managed, and decentralized municipality, which today has an additional quality to it, that of being relocalized. This can hardly be confused with projects that abide by the logic of the institutions and their elections, as is the case of the vast majority of such projects that have sprung up during these last few months. It is worth mentioning that these municipalist projects I'm referring to seem inclined to assume the presence of political forces—Izquierda Unida, Podemos, and many others—that do not, and do not wish to, have any

---

2   Another political movement, sometimes aligned with Podemos, which runs candidates in the municipal elections of various Spanish cities. [editor]

libertarian inclinations. Thus, we cannot even refer to the discussion put forth by the Catalan CUP in its early years, when it decided to run in the municipal elections in small pockets where, at least on paper, an array of direct-democratic forms was conceivable. This is clearly not the sort of horizon invoked by Guanyem Barcelona, Ganemos Madrid, or the majority of the Ganemos that we know.

In these conditions, for once, I believe we have to stand up to the mistakes and manipulations that accompany certain statements and terminological options. It does not seem reasonable—and I need not search for qualifying adjectives here—that once the logic of liberal democracy, representation, and leadership has been criticized, the participation in the elections that the institutions cunningly organize could be shamelessly defended, embellished sometimes with quotes by Proudhon and Kropotkin. The apparent awareness, frequently verbalized, of the shape of the problems to come seems worthless when there is not a single explanation given about how these problems are to be addressed. Although everyone is quite free—why, of course!—to subscribe as one wishes, I firmly believe that the adjective *libertarian*, when applied to these practices and desires, distorts what has always been its common meaning.

In other words, I must base my opinion on the strong assumption that any space won over by self-management is a space lost by the institutions, and vice versa. In concordance with this assumption, the idea that the state is not an enemy of the *commons* seems to me a superstition that cannot gather any consistent data whatsoever in its favor. We could also mention the mirage that invites us to conclude that both self-management and direct action can be defended from an institutional perspective. In the end—and returning to the logic of the parties that dwell in these institutions—the only thing left is to certify that they do not even flirt with the idea of self-management, which is nowhere to be found in the programs defended by Izquierda Unida and Podemos (and, naturally, in the actions of the majority of unions). When short-termism, the acceptance of capitalism as an unquestionable reality, and the objective of employing the state apparatus as a launching pad for a transformative project are imposed, there emerges the social democratic doctrine, which is not, needless to say, self-management.

3.

Let us pay attention now to three debates that revolve, in one way or another, around the previous ones, which reflect likewise the strength of surprisingly common positions and no less surprising omissions. The first of these debates takes the form of an omission, regarding the relation between capital and the state. The reemergence of the superstition that these two are unrelated cannot but be surprising at this stage, to such an extent that some believe the state can be employed, without much ado, for the benefit of liberating and emancipatory projects. Political forces or movements that find shelter in the state do not shape its condition. It is rather the process in the other direction that has been revealed a thousand times in distant and recent history: it is the institutions themselves that end up shaping those who intended, sincerely or insincerely, to make use of them. The inherent logic of representation is a comprehensive device in the service of capital and its interests, with a wide range of consequences in many areas. How is it that those who have maintained a healthy critical reflection about the Spanish *transition* have not realized the key role of elections, and attendant intrigues, in it?[3] I shall stress that am not thinking about the undeniable miseries surrounding the electoral system outlined in 1978; I am referring to the ontological reality of a mechanism that

---

3   As mentioned in chapter 2, *transition* here refers to Spain's transition from dictatorship to a form of liberal democracy. The "democratic" process was shaped by the outgoing authoritarian regime. [editor]

generates the optical illusion that it is the *citizens* themselves, and not the oligarchy and the corporations, who make the important decisions. It also encourages us to conclude that it is enough to vote every four years for the system's rationality to return our cooperation back to us in the form of benefits for all. The idea of rediscovering the supposedly liberating dimension of the rule of law means being at odds with reality: the rule of law is unmistakably subordinated to the interests of capital and its machinery, with no possible liberation from that tutelage.

I shall put it more strongly: whoever thinks that some of our most important problems may be solved without any active response against capitalism and its rules is turning their back on reality for the benefit of preserving something whose rottenness is often quite evident. There are no shortcuts in this terrain: whoever, at this very moment, is incapable of realizing the enormous fiasco of the social democratic proposition is, paradoxically, outside the world in which they think they are firmly inserted. Nothing is left of this proposition, not even the idea of managing capitalism in a civilized manner, if such a thing was ever even remotely possible. And this is not to even mention the ignorance dragged along by social democratic discourse regarding the ecological crisis and its challenges. The thought that we are living on a planet with limited resources is nowhere to be found, and the huge consequences of climate change and the exhaustion of many raw materials that we use are simply forgotten. Our local social democratic economists, by the way, seem unaware that the age of cheap oil has been left very far behind.

Yet renunciations are the order of the day, made by a project that, despite its pretentiousness, has no hold on reality. If, on the one hand, it rises from a fiction, on the other, it does not hesitate to join in the real competition to claim the instruments that represent more of the same. Let us remember that classic social democratic measures—and the unclassic as well—do not question the order of capitalist property and gullibly believe that there might be such a thing as a social and solidarity-based entrepreneurship. They would rather accept the European Union plot, perhaps as a lesser, unavoidable evil—how many more of these will there be?—to which they certainly oppose the very realistic defense of the birth of a "world government." I am not sure if it is of any use to underscore, once more, that they hardly embrace those autonomous, self-managed, and decentralized spaces to which I refer in several sections of this book (and when they do, it is merely rhetorically). Therefore, the vast mythology surrounding the idolized welfare states regains strength, utterly oblivious to what I pointed out before: these are forms of economic and social organization typical and exclusive of capitalism, which hinder the spread of self-management formulas from the bottom up to an unimaginable extent; drink from the moribund philosophy of reformist trade unionism; have not come to liberate, as they announced, so many women, victims of a double or triple exploitation; have no reliable ecological program; and have been useless in mitigating the exploitation and exclusion of so many inhabitants of the global South.

Finally, it often occurs that vindication—our vindication—of direct democracy is met with a response suggesting that it is unfeasible in complex societies like ours. It is worth arguing that we are not simply defending direct democracy: we are reclaiming a radical transformation of society, which in one of its main spheres abides by the aim of allowing the deployment of a non-delegative democracy. As far as I can see, this transformation demands the confluence of at least five verbs: to decrease, to deurbanize, to detechnologize, to depatriarchize, and to decomplexify.

We must *decrease* because we live on a planet with limited resources, and it does not seem that, under such conditions, it would be helpful to place wagers on unlimited growth. We must do it also because in the wealthy global North we have left very far behind all the environmental and resourceful possibilities the earth has to offer. We are also obliged to recover our so-often degraded social life, which we have squandered, engrossed by the logic of production, consumerism, and competitiveness, and bet on other forms of creative leisure against the mercantilization of leisure that is being offered everywhere around us; to distribute work, which is an old syndicalist demand that has miserably died away with time; to reduce the size of many of the productive, administrative, and transportation infrastructures that we use; to revitalize local life in an environment where self-management and direct democracy reemerge; and lastly, to embrace voluntary moderation and simplicity. It is increasingly more evident that the imminent risk of a system collapse requires from us to *deurbanize* and reruralize our societies; that is, to recuperate many of the elements of popular wisdom and self-organization, which over many centuries have marked rural life in a clear standoff against those uninhabitable behemoths our cities represent. We must fight to *detechnologize* our societies or, if it is more agreeable to employ the same argument less radically, to critically weigh whatever emancipatory aspects the system's technology offers us—if such a thing exists, that is. None of the above would make much sense if we do not move on to *depatriarchize* not only the parallel world we desire to build but also the societies we inhabit now, which are unequivocally burdened by values and scenarios unbearable for most women. We must fight, in a nutshell, to *decomplexify* the place we live in; we have accepted ever more complex societies with the apparent paradoxical correlation that we are becoming ever more dependent. We ought to remember what would happen if societies like ours stopped having access to oil supplies: all that we have would come tumbling down overnight.

4.

Those who are firmly convinced that capitalism has entered a stage of terminal corrosion are not the majority. This corrosion translates into an important fact: capitalism has been losing, rapidly and dramatically, many of the brake mechanisms that have allowed it to save some face in the past. The main result is that this collapse is closer than a cursory glance would have us conclude. As we so insistently underscore throughout this book, the terminal corrosion and the collapse become, therefore, essential facts in explaining the urgent need for a reemergence of projects of self-organization and self-management. In other words, if these emancipatory perspectives were not, by themselves, appealing enough, the scenario we are heading toward would make them all the more necessary.

I believe there are two great answers to this collapse. The first, crudely realistic, affirms briefly that there is no other remedy but to wait for the collapse to arrive, for it will be the only way to get the overwhelming majority who inhabit our societies to take heed of reality and of the corresponding duties. Despite its crude realism, this perspective eventually becomes discouraging in unsettling ways: the collapse will translate, by definition, into a spectacular multiplication of the problems and a parallel reduction of our ability to resolve them. The second answer, currently voluntarist—though it enjoys very limited social support—suggests that we must place wagers, once again with urgency, on leaving capitalism as soon as we can. Taking account of our limited abilities, this perspective presupposes today the recuperation of the old project of building parallel societies and thus states that we must fight for an opening of autonomous spaces that, through self-management, demercantilization, and depatriarchization of all relations, sets out to federate or confederate and maintain an open confrontation with the system.

Certainly, our anarchist and anarcho-syndicalist grandfathers or great-grandfathers would not be very pleased with the current outlook of the autonomous spaces. They would have probably embraced it somewhat warily, remembering that the main strategy they proposed to undertake several decades ago was a very different one: that of the expropriation of capital. It is not about us being right and them not quite right. We must acknowledge that it is actually the opposite and that our proposal is the result of a weakness in our movements and efforts, which condemns us, momentarily at least, to gather strengths while we await a different future, with the aggravating result that we are consciously aware that we carry capitalism inside our own heads, so much so that leaving it behind is not exactly a walk in the park.

5.

I reproduce below the content of a text entitled "Por una nueva organización libertaria" ("For a New Libertarian Organization"), which I wrote in December 2014. As you will see, it speaks about the urgent need to articulate, in the current situation we are dealing with right now, a new type of *libertarian* organization, called upon to face the kind of challenges that I have dealt with in this epilogue. It reads as follows:

I believe that in a moment such as the present one—and these are merely my own views—there are many individuals who long for the existence of a libertarian organization that, horizontally and transversally, allows for the reduction of many inherited tensions of the past and paves the way for a stronger intervention upon reality. The urgency in delineating this organization—its foundations seem to be already laid—originates mostly out of changes happening in the emerging sociopolitical scene, characterized by a rising repression, an unsettling demobilization, and the spell that parties, parliaments, and institutions seem to cast upon those who supposedly, until now, had other political inclinations. Yet this urgency eventually emerges from the duties implied by an awareness of the coming terminal corrosion of capitalism and its collapse.

We should also look at the effects of the bubble inside which many have lived during the last few years, a direct result of the belief—unjustified, as we know today—that in May 2011 a new cycle began. Because of that change, separations, hierarchies, and parties were called upon to face an unavoidable crisis, while, at the same time and in direct contradiction, a general commitment to self-management and autonomy was gaining ground. We know now that even if some of that bloomed in the heat of 15-M, the intensity of the process was less than what our desires heralded.

Although some of our comrades suggest, respectably, that we must face the creation of a new organization gradually and cautiously, others believe, with quite convincing arguments, that the situation we are dealing with demands urgency. All in all, though, there do not seem to be great discrepancies regarding the articulating principles of an organization: self-management, direct democracy and action, the rejection of hierarchies and personalisms, and mutual aid (a very good name to give, by the way, to a future organization). These principles address the main aim of contesting liberal pseudo-democracy, the state—in its repressive shape and with its protective aura—and capitalism. And they respond to the certainty that, in a scenario shaped by a resurgence of class struggle, we must also give utmost importance to the members of generations to come and to the other species that walk about this earth with us, as well as to women and to the many inhabitants of the global South, in a project undoubtedly marked by the reaction of developmentalism, patriarchal society, and militarism.

I believe that an essential role ought to be played in this project by those who, without specific *ideological* adherence, have shown a commitment to self-organization, self-management, and autonomy in their day-to-day life. This does not mean marginalizing those who self-identify as anarchists or, in a wider sense, libertarians; it is about including their contributions and shaping an open organization in which, discarding dogmatisms and sectarianisms, the coherence between practices outweighs the rigor of doctrinal adherences. Such an organization would have only one enemy: the system we suffer under in its most diverse manifestations. Under this organization's aegis, no one will ask any anarcho-syndicalist group, libertarian athenaeum, affinity group, self-managed center, or social movement to dissolve itself or to step back. Rather, the nascent organization would provide momentum for such projects.

In addition, it seems that one of this organization's main tasks will consist in defending and amplifying the self-managed, demercantilized, and (it is hoped) depatriarchalized autonomous spaces that have sprung up lately, in a manifest display of what a century ago our ancestors called "propaganda by the deed." But this would only occur if we comprehended that such support would also entail an effort at coordinating and intertwining these spaces and stimulating their confrontational approach against the system.

This brand new organization cannot but have a confederative character. It is inconceivable for directive structures to impose themselves under its wing and for this organization to serve as a launch pad for "liberated" and professional politicians. Its duty is to ultimately demonstrate an international will and, as a result, to do away with the imaginary of states. An initial first step, in line with those lighter ones taken prior to 1936, could very well be to grant this organization an Iberian character, with the possibility of incorporating Portuguese groups that desire to be part of it as well.

The organization that concerns us here ought to have, in short, an important symbolic dimension: that of remembering that we are here and that we are not a narrow minority. But it also ought to work, eventually, on the strengthening of an alternative that would be available in the years to come, when—as will certainly happen—many illusions fall apart. Let us not shy away from our duties in this regard.

INDEX

"Passim" (literally "scattered") indicates intermittent
discussion of a topic over a cluster of pages.